D0727101

1 3 5 7 9 10 8 6 4 2

Vintage
20 Vauxhall Bridge Road,
London SW1V 2SA

Vintage Classics is part of the Penguin Random House
group of companies whose addresses can be found at
global.penguinrandomhouse.com

Penguin
Random House
UK

And The Weak Suffer What They Must? first published by The Bodley Head
in 2016
Adults in the Room first published in by The Bodley Head in 2017
This short edition published by Vintage in 2018

penguin.co.uk/vintage

A CIP catalogue record for this book is available from the British Library

ISBN 9781784874100

Typeset in 9.5/14.5 pt FreightText Pro
by Jouve (UK), Milton Keynes
Printed and bound by Clays Ltd, St Ives plc

Penguin Random House is committed to a sustainable future for our
business, our readers and our planet. This book is made from Forest
Stewardship Council® certified paper.

MIX
Paper from
responsible sources
FSC
www.fsc.org
FSC® C018179

Austerity

YANIS VAROUFAKIS

VINTAGE MINIS

Champion of Austerity

IN SEPTEMBER 2015, after my ministry days were over, I made my first appearance on the BBC's *Question Time*, recorded in front of an audience in Cambridge. Its host David Dimbleby introduced me as Europe's anti-austerity champion, an open invitation to a laddish member of the audience to confront me with his pro-austerity philosophy: 'Economics is really simple. I've got ten pounds in my pocket. If I go out and buy three pints of beer in Cambridge, I'm probably borrowing money. If I carry on doing that, then I'm going to run out of money and I'm going to go bust. It's not difficult.'

One of the great mysteries of life, at least of my life, is how susceptible good people are to this awful logic. In fact, personal finances are a terrible basis for understanding public finance, as I explained in response: 'In your life you have a wonderful independence between your expenses and your income. So when you cut down on your expenses, your income is not cut. But if the country as a whole goes [on] a major savings spree, then its total income is going to come down.'

The reason for this is that at a national level total expenditure and total income are precisely equal because whatever is earned has been spent by someone else. So if every person and business in the country is cutting back, the one thing the state must not do is cut back as well. If it does so, the abrupt fall in total expenditure means an equally abrupt fall in national income, which in turn leads to lower taxes for the Treasury and to austerity's spectacular own goal: an ever-shrinking national income that makes the existing national debt unpayable. This is why austerity is absolutely the wrong solution.

If proof of this were ever needed, Greece has provided it. Our 2010 bailout had two pillars: gigantic loans to fund the French and German banks, and swingeing austerity. To put Greek austerity into perspective: in the two years that followed Greece's 'rescue', Spain, another eurozone country caught up in the same mess, was treated to austerity which amounted to a 3.5 per cent reduction in government expenditure. During the same two-year period, 2010 to 2012, Greece experienced a stupendous 15 per cent reduction in government spending. To what effect? Spain's national income declined by 6.4 per cent while Greece's fell by 16 per cent. In Britain, meanwhile, the newly appointed chancellor George Osborne was championing mild austerity as a means of achieving his dream: a balanced government budget by 2020.[1] Osborne was among the first finance ministers I met after my election. The most startling aspect of that encounter – at least to those in the press who expected a frosty or outright acrimonious meeting – was that we found very little to disagree on. In the first few minutes of our discussion I suggested to him that 'While we may disagree on the merits of austerity, you are not really doing much of it, George, are you?'[2]

He agreed smilingly. How could he not? If an Austerity Olympics had been staged, Greece would have swept the board while Osborne's Britain would have been an also-ran at the bottom of the medals table. Osborne also seemed appreciative of the help he was getting from the Bank of England, which from the moment the City went through its 2008 credit convulsion had printed billions to refloat the banks and keep the economy 'liquid'. Osborne referred to this Bank of England largesse combined with government spending cutbacks as 'expansionary contraction'.

'They are behind me every step of the way,' he told me, evidently relieved not to be in my situation, hostage to a European Central Bank that was doing precisely the opposite.

'I envy you, George,' I lamented. 'Unlike you, I have a central bank stabbing me in the back every step of the way. Can you imagine what it would be like, here in Britain,' I asked, 'if instead of your "expansionary contraction" you were forced, like I am, into a "contractionary contraction"?'

He nodded with a smile, signalling if not solidarity at least sympathy.

That a meeting between a Tory chancellor and a finance minister representing the radical Left in Greece went swimmingly is not actually as puzzling as the press would have everyone believe. Three years previously, with the euro crisis at full blast, a chartered accountants' chamber based in Australia decided to entertain the attendees at their annual conference in Melbourne by staging a debate between a left- and a right-winger from Europe. So they invited Lord (Norman) Lamont, former chancellor in John Major's government, and me to debate, convinced of the fireworks that would ensue. Unfortunately for them, they chose the wrong theme: the eurozone crisis. Having taken the stage in front of a large audience anticipating a cockfight, we quickly discovered that we agreed on almost everything.

The discussion was so amicable, in fact, that after we had left the stage together, we met my wife Danae outside and the three of us proceeded to have lunch together at a riverside restaurant. Bathed in brilliant sunshine, the friendship blossomed – with the help of some delightful Aussie wine, as Norman keeps reminding me. After that we remained in touch, exchanging views in a manner that confirmed we had more in common than even we could have imagined. It was December 2014 when I shocked Norman with the news that I would be taking over Greece's finance ministry within a month. Since that day, and throughout my tumultuous months in office but also beyond, Norman has proved a pillar of strength, a safe friend and a constant supporter. In fact, before I stepped into 11 Downing Street to meet George Osborne in 2015, Norman had called him on the telephone to pave the way for our meeting with a few warm words about me.

While my friendship with Lord Lamont seemed odd to many, especially to my left-wing comrades in government, it fitted well within a broader pattern. Throughout the bleak years, from 2010 to this day, I have been continually stunned by the support that I, a proud leftie, have received from a variety of right-wingers – Wall Street and City of London bankers, right-wing German economists, even US libertarians. To give an example of how weird things got, on a single day in late 2011 I addressed three rather different crowds in New York City – one at Occupy Wall Street, another at the New York Federal Reserve and a third consisting of hedge fund managers and bank reps – and when I told all three audiences the same story about Europe's crisis, I received from each of these three camps of sworn enemies the same warm response.

What authentic libertarians, Wall Street's recovering bankers and Anglo-Celtic right-wingers liked about my otherwise left-wing position was precisely that which the Greek and European establishment loathed: a clear opposition to unsustainable, extend-and-pretend loans that repackage bankruptcy as an illiquidity problem. True-blue free marketeers are allergic to taxpayer-funded benevolence. They reject wholeheartedly my views on the desirability of substantial public investment in recessionary times and of tax-mediated income distribution at all times. But we agree that extending a bankruptcy into the future through taxpayer-funded loans is a horrific waste of resources and a gateway to mass misery. Above all else, libertarians understand debt. As a result, we saw eye to eye on the misanthropic fallacy behind the programme that Christine Lagarde was pushing me, four years later, to embrace.

The official explanation of how the establishment's programme was supposed to help Greece recover in 2015 might be termed 'Operation Restore Competitiveness'. The basic idea was this: Greece has the euro and therefore cannot attract investment from overseas by devaluing its currency, which is the usual strategy for regaining international competitiveness. Instead, it can achieve the same result through what is known as internal devaluation, brought about via massive austerity. How? Swingeing government expenditure cuts will bear down on prices and wages. Greek olive oil, hotel services on Mykonos and Greek shipping fees will therefore become much cheaper for German, French and Chinese customers. With Greece's competitiveness thus restored, exports and tourism will pick up, and with this miraculous transformation investors will rush in, thus stabilizing the economy. In time growth returns and incomes pick up. Job done.

It might have been a convincing argument if it were not

for the elephant in the room – an elephant that libertarians recognize: no sane investor is attracted to a country whose government, banks, companies and households are *all* insolvent at once. As prices, wages and incomes decline, the debt that underlies their insolvency will not fall, it will rise. Cutting one's income and adding new debt can only hasten the process. This is of course what had happened in Greece from 2010 onwards.

In 2010, for every €100 of income a Greek made, the state owed €146 to foreign banks. A year later, every €100 of income earned in 2010 had shrunk to €91 before shrinking again to €79 by 2012. Meanwhile, as the official loans from European taxpayers came in before being funnelled to France and Germany's banks, the equivalent government debt rose from €146 in 2010 to €156 in 2011. Even if God and all the angels were to invade the soul of every Greek tax evader, turning us into a nation of parsimonious Presbyterian Scots, our incomes were too low and our debts too high to reverse the bankruptcy. Investors understood this and wouldn't touch a Greek investment project with a bargepole. The corollary was a humanitarian crisis that ended up bringing people like me into government.

the failure of the establishment, vindicizes.

The Reverse Alchemists

FRANZ WORKED FOR a major German bank for twenty-five years. In November 2011 we sat next to each other on a long-haul flight from Frankfurt to New York. After the first few hours, in which we exchanged a couple of nods and sat in silence, as is typical between strangers, we struck up a conversation about the euro crisis that had begun, in Greece, a year earlier. Within minutes Franz had confided to me that the euro's 'good' years, by which he meant from the late 1990s to just before 2008, had been the worst of his life.

Before 1998 his job had entailed flying around European capitals, assessing the creditworthiness of governments, local authorities, utilities, developers, local banks and large businesses. Prospective borrowers would take him to the nicest restaurants, give long presentations of their business plans, caress his ego, take him to the opera, put on a mixed display of subservience and superiority and, most importantly, make an effort to prove their creditworthiness. Franz would remain non-committal, fly back to Frankfurt and, at his leisure, pore over the data and the documents he had brought back in order to reach a decision as to who got how much of his bank's money. 'Before the euro,' he told me, 'I felt like royalty.'

Things changed abruptly the moment the markets realized that the euro was going to happen and that even Greece would be joining. Around 1998 Franz's charmed life was suddenly transformed into a nightmare. The pressure from his bosses became relentless. 'Lend, lend, lend!' was their new creed. From a relaxed purveyor of scarce money he was transformed into an angst-ridden overpaid proletarian. A weekly quota of loans that he had to make regardless of the creditworthiness of his clients robbed him of the discretion that had previously made him feel important.

The tremendous bonuses he earned for exceeding his lending targets were no compensation, he insisted, for his clients soon realized he was no longer the boss. They were. When Spanish businessmen, Irish developers, Greek bankers, Italian industrialists caught on to the pressure Franz was under to lend to them, their attitude changed. The more strident HQ's orders to unload more of the money sloshing around in their Frankfurt lair became, the cockier they grew. For a time Franz tried to caution the bank's board against the tide of iffy customers the bank would not have touched with a bargepole a little while back. His reports were ignored, and he felt the cold draught of disapproval emanating from his superiors on the odd occasion he spent time in Frankfurt. Soon he realized that his reports clashed with senior management's business plan. He was running a serious risk of being labelled disloyal and an unsafe pair of hands.

In strategic sessions organized to galvanize the workforce around senior management's new logic Franz and his colleagues found that their job descriptions had changed dramatically. They were no longer there to pass judgement on clients. Risk assessment and management had been taken away from them altogether. They were there to peddle loans, to reach their quotas in a manner not dissimilar to encyclopedia salesmen whose salaries depended on how many units they shifted.

'But what about the risk involved?' Franz told me he had once asked. Unlike encyclopedias, which can be ignored by the seller once transferred to the customer, loans have a nasty habit of biting the supplier back. Bankers like Franz had felt important because they were responsible for assessing the riskiness of every loan they granted. It was what gave them their kudos, their sense of self-importance, their mojo. Alas, a new division of labour within banking had brought all this to an end.

People like Franz were now instructed to turn a blind eye to risk. 'Leave risk to our risk managers,' they were told. 'Your job is to chase yield[1] and maximize the sums you lend.' Once the client signed up and received their loan from Franz, the contract was turned over to the risk managers, who would begin a process first developed on Wall Street. Just as in the United States, Franz's loans would be sliced up into small pieces, mixed and matched with slices of other loans, then bundled together into new products, known as derivatives, and sold on to other financial institutions in the four corners of the planet. And so the risk that Franz had created by lending to dodgy Europeans was supposedly dissipated on the vast archipelago of 'riskless' global risk.[2]

Franz's new circumstances were clearly not specific to the eurozone's banks. They were born on Wall Street as a result of the financialization built on the American Minotaur's back, then they made their way to the City of London and to Frankfurt and Paris. What was different about Franz's experience, compared to his colleagues in the Anglosphere, was a particular folly to do exclusively with the form that chasing yield took in the euro area.

Maastricht had declared that monetary union was for ever. To cement this thought, the 1993 treaty specified conditions for entering the single currency but made no provision for exiting. Thus the Hotel California doctrine was enshrined in European law. Once markets had come to believe that no one would ever leave the eurozone, German and French bankers began to look at an Irish or a Greek borrower as equivalent to a German customer of the same creditworthiness. It made sense. If Portuguese, Austrian and Maltese borrowers all made their income in euros, why should they be treated differently? And if the risk involved in lending to particular individuals, firms or governments did not matter, as the loans were dispersed throughout the known universe immediately after being granted, why not treat prospective debtors across the eurozone all the same?

Now that the Greeks and the Italians earned money that could never again be devalued vis-à-vis German money, lending to them appeared to the German and French banks as advantageous as lending to a Dutch or German entity. Indeed, once the euro was invented, it was more lucrative to lend to persons, companies and banks of deficit member states than to German or Austrian customers. This was because in places like Greece, Spain and southern Italy private indebtedness was extremely low. The people were of course generally poorer than Northern Europeans, lived in humbler homes, drove older cars and so on, but they owned their homes outright, had no car loan and usually displayed the deep-seated aversion to debt that recent memories of poverty engender. Bankers love customers with a low level of indebtedness and some collateral in the form of a farmhouse or an apartment in Naples, Athens or Andalusia. Once the fear of devaluation of the lira, the drachma or the peseta in their pocket passed, these became the customers that bankers like Franz were instructed to target.

Franz went to some lengths to impress upon me the suddenness and force with which his bank targeted the European periphery. Its new business plan was straightforward: to secure a higher share of the eurozone market than other banks, the French banks in particular, which were also on a lending spree. This meant one thing: lend to the deficit countries, which offered the bankers a triptych of advantages.

First, the low levels of private indebtedness left enormous room for a lot more lending. Back-of-the-envelope calculations made French and German bankers salivate at the scope for loans in the Mediterranean, in Portugal and in Ireland. In contrast to British or Dutch clients, who were mortgaged up to their ears and in a position to borrow little or nothing more, Greek and Spanish customers could quadruple their borrowing, given that they had so little debt to begin with. Second, the surplus nations' exports to deficit countries welcomed into the euro were now immune to devaluations of the defunct, weaker currencies. In what the bankers considered a virtuous circle, their increasing loans to deficit nations foreshadowed more domestic growth, which in turn justified the loans they were extending to them. Third, German bankers drooled over the difference between the interest rate they could charge to German customers and the going rate in places like Greece. The chasm between the two was a direct consequence of the countries' trade imbalance. A large trade surplus means that cars and washing machines flow from the surplus to the deficit country with cash flowing the opposite way. The surplus country becomes awash with 'liquidity' – with cash accumulating in proportion to the net exports pouring into its trading partner. As the supply of cash increases within the surplus nation's banks – in Frankfurt to be precise – it becomes more readily available and therefore cheaper to borrow. In other words, its price drops. And what is the price of money? The interest rate! Thus interest rates in Germany were much lower than in Greece, Spain and their equivalents, where the outflow of cash as the Greeks and the Spanish purchased more and more Volkswagens maintained the price of euros in Europe's south above its equivalent in Germany.[3]

It was this burgeoning chasm of lending interest rates between the eurozone's core and the periphery countries that wrecked Franz's life, for his task was to lend wherever he could charge the highest interest rate – chasing yield. The euro's creation had inadvertently saturated the German banks with liquidity that men like Franz were then forced by their bosses to re-export to every nook and cranny of the deficit nations – nations typified by a hitherto low level of indebtedness. Franz's mission was to boost debt in the deficit countries for the purpose of reaping the huge rewards that were springing from the chasm between interest rates in the weaker and stronger eurozone nations.

Towering above all other lending, courtesy of the larger sums involved, was public debt – the borrowing of governments. Even a small difference between the interest rates bankers charged the Greek state relative to the

German government was a licence to print money. As long as the assumption held that the monetary union was for ever, these differences in interest rates – known as spreads – ensured that a banker taking money out of Germany or France (at a rate of, say, 3.5 per cent) and lending it to the Greek state (at, say 4 per cent) would make a risk-free profit. How much? The difference between the two rates (0.5 per cent) multiplied by the amount lent to the Greek government. But the more money lent to the Greek government (or the Irish banks for that matter) the lower the spread[4] and therefore the more loans the banker had to shift in order to maintain his profits. 'Frenzy' is probably too mild a word to convey what was going on.

'I lived the life of a predator lender' were Franz's words as the plane touched down. Picking up our hand luggage we headed for the customs area. Franz shook my hand, adding, 'Greece was our sub-prime market. Good luck, mate.' Little did either of us know that four years later I would be struggling to explain to my fellow finance ministers that Greece's unpayable debt was a symptom of collective eurozone folly.

Nein cubed

It is September 2008. Dick Fuld, Lehman Brothers' last CEO, begs Hank Paulson, the US treasury secretary, for a gigantic credit line to keep Lehman afloat. Paulson famously turns him down. The best he can do, he tells Fuld, is to ask other investment bankers to help shoulder some of Lehman's bad trades. But that's all: no bailout. 'File for bankruptcy, if you must.'

Imagine a slightly different, entirely fictional, exchange in which the US treasury secretary were to say to Fuld, 'No bailout for you and you are not allowed to file for bankruptcy!' What? Surely a figure of authority cannot demand of a bankrupted entity that it refrain from insolvency while at the same time denying it a bailout. It couldn't happen. Except that it did happen. Not in the United States, of course, but in Europe eighteen months later.

Towards the end of 2009 George Papandreou, the newly elected Greek prime minister, had all the indications that Greece was another Lehman Brothers. By January 2010 there was no doubt left: the Greek state stood no chance of servicing its gigantic debt of more than €300 billion. Locked into the eurozone, there was no drachma to devalue and no Greek central bank to assist. Desperate for a bailout before markets and citizens became fully aware of the situation, he contacted Greece's European partners for help. There were two key people with the capacity to answer his distress call: Chancellor Angela Merkel of Germany and Jean-Claude Trichet, a Frenchman presiding over the European Central Bank who was terribly keen to maintain the French elites' pretence that France and Germany spoke with one voice and shared a single agenda on matters monetary.

Merkel's answers, enthusiastically seconded by Trichet, will go down in history: *nein* to a bailout for Greece, *nein* to interest rate relief[5] and, stupefyingly, *nein* to Greece defaulting on its debts Lehman-style. Denial has never appeared more vividly nor been delivered with greater aplomb. The leader of a bankrupt country, whose currency was issued in Frankfurt and controlled by Mr Trichet, was instructed by the German chancellor not even to think of declaring bankruptcy, even as he was being denied assistance.

The Greece–Lehman analogy is justified in a number of ways, despite the fact that one is a country and the other a defunct merchant bank. Both Lehman and Greece were bound to collapse as soon as financialization got into trouble. Tasked with feeding the American Minotaur's enormous appetite for the surplus nations' exports and money, financialization was certain to experience a sharp reversal once the mountain of derivatives it had built reached a tipping point. Like a vicious tide that turns without warning, credit and money disappeared from America's and Europe's financial circuits. Deprived of the piles of private money the financiers conjured up daily, the entities with the greatest burden of debt would be the first ones to crash. Lehman and Greece were the most famous of them, but behind the headlines, and beyond the tragic figures of Mr Fuld and Mr Papandreou, something larger and more terrible was unfolding: the certainties upon which the eurozone had been erected were about to be revealed as illusions. The German chancellor's triple *nein* to Mr Papandreou summed up the determination with which Europe's establishment denied the truth about the eurozone: that it was the one globally significant macro-economy least prepared to sustain the shock waves of this most violent *fin de siècle*.

Subterfuge

Financialization's house of cards (or derivatives, to be precise) began to collapse in 2007, under the weight of its hubris. With private money minting winding down, as the bankers no longer trusted each other's paper products, liquidity dried up fast everywhere. The first bank run hit Britain's Northern Rock, and the first taxpayer-funded bailout – of US investment bank Bear Stearns – followed. American officials like Paulson, Fed chairman Ben Bernanke and New York Fed chief Timothy Geithner began frantically trying to contain the contagion. In the course of the next twelve months they authorized the manufacture of as much public money as they deemed necessary with which to replace the private money disappearing from the system. But how many of their banker friends should they rescue, and whom should they abandon to the raging market forces? In September 2008 they opted for a nuanced response.

They would allow one bank, Lehman, to fail as a morality tale for the rest of the bankers and as a signal to the

American people that their public officials were not entirely under the banks' spell. Meanwhile, they were preparing to bail out all other financial institutions if Lehman's insolvency got out of hand. The result was the largest ever transfer of private losses from banks' books onto the public debt ledger.

Wall Street's troubles instantly infected the City of London, and the Anglosphere went from financial supremacy to global basket case. Officials in Brussels, Paris, Frankfurt and Berlin rejoiced, confident that the Anglos, who had been lecturing them on the flimsiness of Europe's monetary union and social market model, had got their comeuppance. Until, that is, they realized that Germany's and France's banks were in a state worse than Lehman, with their asset books weighed down with US-sourced derivatives that had lost 99 per cent of their value.

Germany's federal government panicked. In 2009 the Bundestag, Germany's federal parliament, was bamboozled into setting aside €500 billion of credits and transfers to save German bankers. Similar action was taken in France, where the top four financial institutions faced immediate obliteration. Parliamentarians in both nations were told in no uncertain terms: cough up ridiculous sums for the banks or the world as you know it comes to an end.

And so it was that politicians used to quibbling over a few million euros to be spent on pensioners, health or education gave their governments carte blanche to transfer hundreds of billions to bankers hitherto awash with liquidity. This helped Germany and France's banks survive the collapse of their foolish derivative trades. However, another calamity beckoned: the loans that bankers, like Franz, had granted to the deficit regions of the eurozone were sizeable enough to bankrupt those nations if stressed Irish, Spanish, Greek banks were to default. Before the ink of the first agreements had dried, a second bank bailout was in progress: a bailout for the bankers of deficit countries whose governments could not afford to rescue them.

France and Germany's governments were loath to go back to their parliaments to ask for fresh money for Irish, Italian, Spanish and Greek banks, so the task was passed on to the European Central Bank. Lacking the powers that a proper central bank ought to have, the ECB allowed the eurozone's banks to do something remarkably dicey: issue IOUs that no one would want to buy[6] (given that the banks were insolvent), take these IOUs to their government's finance minister, have the minister stamp on the IOUs a state guarantee (which everyone knew the state could not honour) and finally have the banks deposit these IOUs back with the ECB as collateral in exchange for money that the ECB created to lend to them.

In effect, the eurozone's central bank, whose Maastricht-era charter bans it from lending to member-state governments or to insolvent banks, was lending indirectly to the government of each deficit nation the money its insolvent banks required to pretend they were not insolvent.[7] The banks thus pretended to be solvent; the deficit states pretended they had the money to guarantee that the banks were solvent; and the ECB stood by, pretending that these sad pairs of insolvent banks and insolvent states were perfectly solvent and thus eligible under the ECB's charter for ECB liquidity.

The strangest ritual I had to endure during my five months as Greece's minister of finance in the first half of 2015 concerned this shenanigan almost eight years after it was first invented. My most trusted aide and good friend Wasily Kafouros would come to my office bearing the contracts according to which my ministry, and by extension the Greek state, was guaranteeing IOUs on behalf of Greece's bankers. Mindful of my contempt for this arrangement, Wasily would approach me with the utmost care and only at times he deemed relatively stress free. Both of us shook with rage at the sad fact that my signatures were guaranteeing more than €50 billion of private bank debt while our state could not rub together a few hundred million euros to pay for our public hospitals, our schools or Greece's old-age pensioners.

Placing my signature on these pieces of paper, week in and week out, was probably the oddest and at once the ugliest thing I had to do. The closest rival for the title of Most Disagreeable Ministerial Chore was the obligatory repetition of the lie that Greece's banks were solvent and that the government would honour all its commitments to every one of its creditors, including the guarantees that I was signing in the full knowledge that I could not honour them if the need arose. My only solace was that I was not alone: eurozone finance ministers and central bankers all over the continent had been engaged in this type of gross subterfuge since the heady days of the fall of 2008.[8]

Denial

The reason Greece became the first eurozone country to go manifestly bankrupt was simple. From the moment it looked likely that the drachma was history and Greece's place in the euro was safe, bankers like Franz had gone into a frenzy of lending for the reasons he explained to me so eloquently as we were flying to New York.

The part of the story that Franz left out, probably because he had missed its significance, was the labour market measures – known as the Hartz reforms[9] – that the German Federal Republic enacted as soon as euro notes began to circulate. Implemented at a time of US-led growth, these reforms aimed at enhancing German exports and their competitiveness by making them cheaper through reducing German workers' average take-home pay significantly, both by cutting hourly wage rates and pushing large numbers of workers into so-called mini-jobs.[10]

The result was that German workers, as their share of

their employers' profits fell, could not afford the goods they produced. Deprived of domestic demand, surplus German products thus flowed to places like Ireland, Greece and Spain, where demand for them was supported by the loans Franz and his Frankfurt banker colleagues, dipping into the German corporate profit glut, had shifted to Europe's periphery. The export of German goods and German profits to the rest of the eurozone created debt-fuelled annual growth of 5 per cent in Greece and Ireland, making these fragile deficit-ridden societies look like miracle economies, in contrast to Germany growing at a feeble 1 per cent.

Is it any wonder that financially stressed German workers visiting Greece in the summer months rubbed their eyes at the sight of rising living standards they could only dream of? And is it surprising that when the German loan-driven bubble burst in Europe's south, this bewilderment turned into hostility towards Greece, Spain and Italy's grasshoppers? Of course what the German tourists never saw was that Greece was full of hard-working ants struggling to survive during those years of miraculous growth. Low-wage workers and pensioners were being told that they'd never had it so good – that their real wages and living standards were rising – only they did not feel that way. And they were right.[11] Whereas richer Greeks, who lived well off the back of German and French bank loans, prospered, poorer Greeks fell increasingly into a poverty trap. In the good times! And when the bad times came in 2010 they were told that they had been profligate grasshoppers who had caused the crisis and now had to pay the price.

Many ask: did the authorities in Brussels, Berlin and Athens not recognize that Greek public debt (and the rich Greeks' lifestyle) was unsustainable? The startling answer is that they did not, and here is why. If you think of a nation's public debt and its national income as two growing mountains, debt appears manageable as long as the income mountain grows at a greater pace than the debt mountain. The debt mountain grows automatically as interest piles up on top of it at a rate equal to the interest rate. In Greece that rate had fallen to 3 per cent, courtesy of the foreign-sourced lending spree. At the same time, the national income mountain (measured in euros) was growing much faster, at 8 per cent – 3 per cent of this growth due to rising prices and 5 per cent resulting from higher production. Thus it seemed that Greece's public debt, while large, was serviceable owing to much faster rising incomes. But when the events of 2008 spread the credit crunch, two terrible things happened at once that put paid to this illusion.

First, the almost complete cessation of new credit meant that the Greek state could no longer refinance its debt unless it was prepared to pay the few risk-loving investors left in the money markets interest rates exceeding 10 per cent. Second, Greek national income went into reverse growth, falling because of a global recession that depressed tourism and the incomes of the countless Greeks trading in debt-financed imports. When the debt mountain's growth rate – the interest rate – shot up from 3 to 10 per cent and the income mountain instead of growing started shrinking (first by –3 per cent, then by –5 per cent), Greece's debt sustainability became a contradiction in terms.

Against these brutal facts, the triple *nein* in reply to George Papandreou's request for help in early 2010 was devastating in its inanity. It was as realistic as suggesting to him that he ought to beam Greece up to another galaxy where it was possible to avoid declaring bankruptcy without devaluation, without debt relief and without new loans. The triple *nein* was a knee-jerk expression of Europe's denial that it was facing a structural crisis. It had created a monetary union featuring states without a central bank to back them at a time of global crisis and a European Central Bank without a state watching its back. The Maastricht rules were impossible to abide by.

The triple *nein* held from January 2010 until May of that year, when at last Berlin and Frankfurt could no longer avoid the fact that Greece was about to default on its debts to German and French banks. At that point Europe's denial mutated into another form: into Greece's so-called bailout, which was to become the blueprint for equivalent action in Dublin, Lisbon and Madrid and which left its mark on Rome, even on the Netherlands and on France, pushing the whole continent into a new recessionary phase.[12] The gist of the deal offered to Greece was simple: as you are now insolvent, we shall grant you the largest loan in history on condition that you shrink your national income by an amount never seen since the grapes of wrath. It would take a smart eight-year-old to see that such a bailout could not end well.

But this was not a bailout. Greece was never bailed out. Nor were the rest of Europe's swine – or the PIIGS, as Portugal, Ireland, Italy, Greece and Spain became collectively branded. Greece's bailout, then Ireland's, then Portugal's, then Spain's were primarily rescue packages for French and German banks.

In bending its rules to rescue the PIIGS's private banks with the issue of the aforementioned IOUs, the ECB had given Chancellor Merkel and France's President Nicolas Sarkozy some respite from having to go back to their parliaments for more taxpayers' money for French and German bankers. But much more was now needed. By May 2010 Greek government bonds had lost 82 per cent of their value. Put differently, a bank or private investor owed 100 euros by the Greek state could only sell this debt on for 18 euros. This was a disaster for those French and German banks that were owed up to €200 billion by Greece. It was also only the tip of a huge iceberg. In 2009 the exposure of German banks to Greek, Irish, Spanish, Portuguese and Italian debt amounted to a dizzying €704 billion.[13] Much, much more than the total capital base of Germany's banking system. If Greece went under, and contagion brought down some of the other peripheral banks, Germany's banking system would be toast.

Suddenly it became imperative to save Greece. But with the Greek state cut off from money markets, as no sane investor would lend to the Athens government, the German and French banks feared the worst: Greece would have to default, and the banks would be at the mercy of regulators whose rules said they had to declare the insolvency of venerable banks like BNP Paribas or Finanz Bank. Another German and French bank bailout had become unavoidable. The second one in less than two years.

The problem was that Chancellor Merkel and President Sarkozy could not imagine going back to their parliaments for more money for their banker chums, so they did the next best thing: they went to their parliaments invoking the cherished principle of solidarity with Greece, then with Ireland, then Portugal and finally Spain. Thus Mr Papandreou was pushed into accepting the largest loan in history, of which the bulk, more than 91 per cent, went to prop up the French and German banks by buying back from them at a hundred euros bonds whose market value had declined to less than twenty euros.

A cynical ploy that transferred hundreds of billions of losses from the books of French and German banks to Europe's taxpayers was presented to the world as the manifestation of European solidarity. What makes this transfer sinister rather than just cynical was that the

Greek loan came not only from French and German tax-payers but also from the Portuguese, the Slovaks, the Irish – from taxpayers whose banks had nothing to gain. In essence, the private losses of French and German banks were spread throughout the eurozone, forcing even the weakest citizens of the weakest of member states to chip in.

The Greek bailout did not go down well in the sixteen parliaments where it was discussed. Nationalists and anti-Europeans grabbed the opportunity to lambast their governments for daring to ask the people to cough up money for the worst of the Mediterranean's grasshoppers when they themselves were suffering from the post-2008 recession. Behind the scenes the governments would inform them that the Greek bailout was all about saving their own banks, but the opportunity for putting on a show of patriotism was too tempting to ignore. So they demanded to see some Greek blood before signing off on the deal.

The Greek loan thus came with vicious strings attached – strings designed to cause visible pain to the weakest Greeks. The conditionalities, as the strings were called, boiled down to the dismantling of basic social welfare provisions, this to be supervised by officials representing the ECB, the European Commission and the International Monetary Fund.[14] Thus the troika – the triumvirate of the ECB, the EC and the IMF – was born. It comprised a small group of bailiffs, disguised as

technocrats, who acquired powers that Europe's g
ments cannot dream of. With every visitation o
troika, the dream of shared European prosperity was
dealt another blow.

Fiscal waterboarding

My use of the term fiscal waterboarding back in 2010 was,
after I became finance minister in 2015, used as evidence
that I was a provocateur. In fact it was a perfectly apt and
reasonable term by which to describe the troika's practices in Athens and elsewhere. What does waterboarding
involve? You take a subject, lay him on his back and engulf
his head with water so that he suffocates. Just before he
dies, you stop, you allow the subject to take a few agoniz-
ing breaths, and then you start again. You repeat until he
confesses.

Fiscal waterboarding is obviously not physical, it's fiscal. But the idea is the same, and it is exactly what
happened to successive Greek governments from 2010
onwards. Instead of air, Greek governments nursing
unsustainable debts were starved of liquidity. At the same
time they were banned from defaulting to creditors.
Facing payments they were being forced to make, they
were denied liquidity till the very last moment, just before
formal bankruptcy. Instead of confessions, they were
forced to sign further loan agreements, which they knew
would add new impetus to the crisis. The troika would

provide just enough liquidity in order to repay its own members. Exactly like waterboarding, the liquidity provided was calculated to be just enough to keep the subject going without defaulting formally, but never more than that. And so the torture continued with the government kept completely under the troika's control.

This is fiscal waterboarding, and I cannot imagine a better and more accurate term to describe what has been going on since 2010. During my five months in the finance ministry I came to know this most interesting process at first hand. Such as, for instance, when the European Central Bank connived to reduce our government's access to liquidity by preventing Greece's banks from purchasing our treasury bills.

Of course the problem with waterboarding is that it is a poor method of eliciting the truth, as subjects will confess to anything the interrogator wants to hear to stop the torture. So it was with the troika's fiscal waterboarding. Successive governments of indebted eurozone member states agreed to the troika's programmes even though they knew they would deepen the crises.

Ponzi austerity

Franz and his banker colleagues had been, in effect, running a huge Ponzi scheme in the deficit nations of Europe's monetary union. This is what Franz meant with his sad admission, 'I lived the life of a predator lender.' And when the pyramid crumbled, as Ponzi schemes inevitably do, Ponzi growth metamorphosed into what I once called Ponzi austerity.

Standard Ponzi schemes are based on a sleight of hand that creates the appearance of a fund whose overall value is growing faster than the value of the investments made in it. In reality the opposite is true. The fraudster behind a Ponzi scheme usually helps himself to some of the incoming capital, but the fund is not creating any new capital with which to replenish these leakages, let alone pay the returns it has promised. Any dividends paid to maintain the illusion of growth come from new investments. And this appearance of growth that does not really exist is, of course, the lure that brings into the scheme new participants, whose capital is utilized by the Ponzi scheme's operator to maintain that facade.

Ponzi austerity is the inverse of Ponzi growth. Whereas Ponzi growth schemes are based on the lure of a growing fund, in the case of Ponzi austerity the attraction is the promise of debt reduction for the purposes of defeating insolvency through a combination of austerity belt-tightening and new loans that provide the bankrupt with necessary funds to repay maturing debts, such as bonds. As it is impossible to escape insolvency in this way, given austerity's depressing effect on income, Ponzi austerity schemes, just like Ponzi growth schemes, necessitate a constant influx of new loans to maintain the illusion that bankruptcy has been averted. But to attract these loans, the Ponzi austerity's operators must do their utmost to maintain the facade of deficit reduction.

Ponzi growth has been around for ages. But it took the collective wisdom of Europe's great and good to create history's first Ponzi austerity scheme. The Greek, Portuguese, Irish, Spanish and Cypriot loan agreements are splendid examples. Bankrupted states, in a death embrace with bankrupted banking sectors, were forced to take on ever-increasing loans (mainly from European taxpayers) on condition of belt-tightening austerity. As the scheme progressed and more loans were agreed, public debt as a proportion of national income only rose. Again, as in Ponzi growth schemes, where more and more investments are required to maintain the pretence of growth, in the case of Greece, Portugal, Ireland, Spain and Cyprus more and more loans were necessary in order to maintain the pretence of debt reduction.

Here is an example of eurozone-style Ponzi austerity at its worst. It is spring 2012. The Greek government that signed up to the country's second bailout[15] has collapsed under popular anger at the nation's sad state. A fresh election is due in May 2012, and Syriza, a radical left-wing party that advocates rescinding the bailout agreement, is rising fast in the polls. Horrified at the prospect of an anti-troika party in government, the troika suspends the disbursement of loan payments to the interim Greek government.[16] The administration is left with no alternative other than to suspend its own payments to institutions and individuals. Hospitals, schools, wages, pensions all suffer. But the concern of the great and the good is about Greece's debt to the European Central Bank – the ECB.

You see, dear reader, in 2010 an ill-fated attempt to shore up Greek government bonds by the ECB's president, Monsieur Jean-Claude Trichet, involved the purchase by the ECB of a tranche of Greek bonds at low, low prices. The stated objective was to prop up their value and thus help prevent the Greek state from losing its market access – its capacity to borrow from private investors.[17] Trichet's ploy failed, as did Greece.[18] Regardless, the ECB holds these bonds, which start maturing. Had they not been purchased by the ECB in 2010, they would have been 'given a haircut' (written down) together with the rest of the Greek government's bonds in private hands a few months earlier, in early 2012. But no, the ECB cannot accept write-downs from member states because it is against its charter, which prohibits it from doing anything that resembles financing member states – except, of course, when it bends its own rules in order to rescue assorted bankers, as we saw earlier.[19]

This means that the caretaker Greek government, while putting Greece's social economy through the wringer, has to find €5 billion in a few days to repay the ECB for one of these maturing bonds. Where will the money come from? The troika has suspended loan payments and no privateer is ready to go where even the troika refuses to tread.

The obvious thing to do under the circumstances is for Athens to default on the bonds that the ECB owns or for the ECB to offer the Greek government longer maturities, a debt swap or something of the sort. But this is something that Frankfurt and Berlin reject with venom. When it comes to countries like Germany and France, the rules are meant to be broken.[20] But for countries like Greece the rules are the rules are the rules! Even if they are unworkable and unenforceable. The Greek state can default against the weakest of Greek and non-Greek citizens, against pension funds and the like, but its debts to the ECB are sacrosanct. They have to be paid come what may. But how?

This is what they come up with in lieu of a solution: the ECB allows the Greek government to issue worthless IOUs – short-term treasury bills – that no private investor will touch, and pass them on to the insolvent Greek banks.[21] The Greek banks then hand over these IOUs to the European System of Central Banks[22] as collateral in exchange for loans that the banks give back to the Greek government so that Athens could repay the ECB.

If this sounds like a Ponzi scheme it is because it is the mother of all Ponzi schemes, a merry-go-round of Ponzi austerity which left both the insolvent banks and the insolvent Greek state a little more insolvent while the Greek population sank deeper and deeper into despair. And all so the European Union could pretend that its inane rules had been respected.

If this sounds like a Ponzi scheme it is because it is the mother of all Ponzi schemes

This is but one example of the vicious cycle of Ponzi austerity replicated incessantly throughout the eurozone. Its stated purpose was to reduce debt. But debt rose everywhere.[23] Is this a failure? Yes and no. It is a failure in terms of Brussels's stated objectives but not in terms of the underlying motives. For the true purpose of the bail-out loans was to effect a transfer of the periphery's bad debts from the books of the (mainly) Northern European banks to the shoulders of Europe's taxpayers at the cost of increasing debts and a recession caused by the conditions attached to the new loans.

These toxic transfers, effected in the name of European solidarity, led to a death dance of insolvent banks and bankrupt states, sad couples sequentially marched off the cliff of competitive austerity. Deflation, ultra-low investment, social fragmentation and rising poverty ensured that large sections of proud European populations, mostly the weakest of their citizenry, were dragged into the contemporary equivalent of the Victorian poorhouse.

Falling dominoes or tumbling mountaineers?

It was 2011. The contagion of default and collapse was spreading via the common currency from country to country. As the Greek disease spread, infecting Ireland, Portugal and Spain, before reaching Italy and threatening to bring the

whole house of cards down, the metaphor of falling domi-
noes became rather oversubscribed in the media. A better
analogy would be that of a mountaineering club.

Imagine a group of disparate mountaineers perched on
some steep cliff face, some of them more agile, others less
fit, all bound together in a forced state of solidarity by a
single rope. Unbelievably, the members of our mountaineering club abide by an irrevocable rule: the common rope
is never pinned to the rock face they are climbing. Suddenly an earthquake hits (such as the collapse of Wall
Street), and one of them (of, let's say, a Hellenic disposition) is dislodged, her fall arrested only by the rope.
Under the strain of the stricken member's weight, dan-
gling in midair, and with some especially loose rocks
falling from above, the next-weakest mountaineer (Irish
perhaps?) struggles to hang on but eventually has to let go
too.

The strain on the remaining mountaineers greatly
increases, and the new next-weakest member is now tee-
tering on the verge of a fall that will cause another hideous
tug on the remaining line of saviours. Will the stronger
members hold on? Will they manage to reach the peak,
carrying the hangers-on with them, before the ruthless
pull of gravity plunges the whole group into the ravine
below? Or will the strongest members cut themselves
loose with their knives (and revert to something akin to
the Deutsche Mark)?

The reason why the mountaineering analogy is far

better than the domino metaphor has to do with the euro-zone's architecture and in particular the Maastricht rule that no member state should count on financial aid from other member states or from the union – the so-called 'no bailout' clause that was meant to deter governments from getting into trouble in the first place.[24] Could this rule (the equivalent of not pinning the common rope to the cliff) be respected while at the same time prohibiting countries like Greece from declaring bankruptcy and defaulting on the bankers? Ordinary minds would answer in the negative. But Brussels functionaries are not ordinary people.

Aided ably by financial consultants who had made a fortune out of bending logic to their advantage, they came up with an ingenious alternative. They created a new fund, which they called the European Financial Stability Facility (EFSF), to bail out the fallen member states, lending them the money necessary to make the bankers whole. It was the financial equivalent of binding our mountaineers more tightly together but still without pinning the common rope to the cliff face.

The trick that allowed member states to lend to other stricken members while still apparently respecting the 'no bailout' clause was hidden in the devilish structure of the bonds that the EFSF would issue. At the beginning, when only Greece needed bailout money of, say, €1 billion, the EFSF would issue a bond with a face value of €1 billion, sell it to the money markets and pass the money on to the Greek government, which would promptly pass it on to Europe's bankers. The €1 billion liability now fell upon Greece but was backed by the eurozone member states that remained solvent, which had suddenly become Greece's creditors, each one of them bearing a proportion of this new debt equal to its relative national income.[25] To preserve the 'no bailout' clause and to ensure that there was no common debt whatsoever – that every euro of debt belonged to one and only one member state – the slice of that €1 billion bond belonging to, say, France would bear a rate of interest payable to the bond's owner (the investor that purchased it) equal to the interest rate France paid to borrow for its own purposes. The Spanish slice would bear a different interest rate, so too the Italian, and so on.

So each nation participating in Greece's rescue, or later in Portugal's, Ireland's and the rest, paid market interest rates depending on its own creditworthiness, which reflected its country-specific risk of bankruptcy. This meant that the member state with the highest probability of going Greece's way paid most interest for the slice of the EFSF bond it guaranteed so that Greece could receive the €1 billion of new debt.

Those familiar with the structured derivatives that brought down Lehman Brothers and Wall Street along with it – so-called collateralized debt obligations, or CDOs – will recognize in the EFSF bailout bonds the same form of synthesized risk. Except that the EFSF bonds were even more toxic than Wall Street's noxious derivatives! To see this, consider what happened when Ireland went bankrupt and needed an EFSF-funded bailout.

The EFSF had to issue new debt to lend to Ireland on behalf of all the eurozone countries except Greece, which had already fallen into insolvency, and of course Ireland. This meant that, with Greece and Ireland out of the group of creditor nations, a greater burden had to be shared by the remaining EFSF members. The markets immediately focused on the next marginal country, the one currently borrowing at the highest interest rates within the EFSF in order to loan money to the fallen Greece and Ireland: Portugal. Immediately, Portugal's own interest rates shot up, pushing it over the edge.

This would continue until the band of nations within the EFSF became so small it was either unable or unwilling to bear the burden of the fallen states' combined debt. At that point, led by Germany, the remaining solvent nations would have to signal the euro's bitter end and withdraw. Or the ECB would have to invent another trick to violate its impossible rulebook.

Ponzi austerity spreads

At the end of 2011 ECB president Jean-Claude Trichet, arguably the world's worst central banker, was replaced by Mario Draghi, a frightfully smart former chair of Italy's treasury and central bank and, not insignificantly, a former Goldman Sachs International vice president. Draghi could see that his own country had only a few months left before falling into the same rut as Greece, leading to Spain and France's incapacity to service their multi-trillion-euro debts. In effect, the euro was about to dissolve as the eurozone's mountaineering club members toppled sequentially, and in slow motion, into the abyss. So Draghi decided to take immediate action.

His first move, a couple of weeks after taking over the ECB's helm, was to 'print' a trillion euros and lend them to the eurozone's stricken banks. As long as the bankers could find some sheets of paper lying around, Draghi would accept them as collateral and hand over the cash.[26] As is Europe's habit, this simple operation was given a complex name, Long Term Refinancing Operations. Draghi's real intention with the LTRO was to lend to the banks for next to no interest so that the banks would, in turn, do what the ECB's charter did not allow him to do: lend to the faltering states, in particular to the Italian government, which was on its way to the poorhouse.

Meanwhile the concept of a democracy-free zone, which had begun life in Brussels in the 1950s, had just been given a new twist in Rome, and indeed Athens. Two prime ministers, George Papandreou in Greece and the inimitable Silvio Berlusconi in Italy, had been deemed by Chancellor Merkel (with France's President Sarkozy in tow) unfit to maintain the pace of austerity necessary to justify in the Bundestag the propping up of Italy's and

Greece's unsustainable debts either via the EFSF or the ECB. It is hard to believe that prime ministers of European nations can be pushed aside or selected at the whim of another European leader, but this is exactly what happened when Papandreou was replaced by the ECB's former vice president, a certain Mr Loukas Papademos, and Silvio Berlusconi by Mario Monti, a former European commissioner.[27]

Monti's mission was to set Italy's public finances in some kind of order. He knew that Berlin was keen to put Italy through the same ordeal as Greece, with the hated troika invading Rome's ministries and imposing hyper-austerity. So he tried to prevent this by introducing a milder form of austerity himself, hoping to contain Italy's debt before going to the Eurogroup cap in hand. In this latter task, he looked to the other Mario, the ECB's Mr Draghi, for badly needed help. It was to arrive in the form of the aforementioned LTRO trick.

At the time all Europe's banks were on the verge of collapse, while front-line states like Italy were faring just as badly. The ECB hoped that its LTRO loans, at almost zero interest, would net the borrowing banks a nice little profit from lending the money on to the states at higher interest rates which would nevertheless be far, far lower than the usurious rates private investors were demanding from those same governments. Both banks and states would thus be reprieved, at least for a while.

One morning in February 2012 the CEO of one of

Italy's largest banks informed Monti's government that his bank would fail unless it received €40 billion there and then. A state that was about to collapse under its own debt burden, Greek style, was thus put in an awful dilemma: fork out a sum it could not afford or sit idly by as the nation's banks closed their doors one after the other. Thankfully Draghi's LTRO was at hand. So this is what happened: the failing bank issued IOUs worth €40 billion on that very morning that no investor would buy, given the bank's parlous state. The Italian minister of finance guaranteed this private debt by committing future taxes to it, thereby adding €40 billion to Italy's public debt. Finally, the bank took these IOUs to the ECB and received cash from Mr Draghi's generous LTRO programme.

So, at the end of the proverbial day, Draghi's plan to prop up the Italian banks and the Italian state had failed. Instead, his scheme was supporting the banks but had plunged the Italian state deeper into unsustainable debt.

Despotism

Mr Klaus Masuch was until recently the ECB's representative in the troika delegation that spreads panic everywhere it goes. In early 2012 the troika passed through Dublin. At the press conference after his meeting with Irish officials Mr Masuch felt comfortable enough among mostly sycophantic journalists to relate his view that the Irish people were sophisticated because they understood that the troika's endeavours were tough but necessary. His precise words were: 'The attitude [of the Irish people] as far as I can see, and I have a limited perspective, is very good. I am impressed by the depth of the discussion in Ireland and by the understanding of complex financial and economic arguments . . . When I come from the airport by taxi the taxi drivers are very well informed, so I think this is a very good sign that here we have an open discussion. It's a difficult adjustment process but there is an economic debate and this is how it should be.'

At which point Vincent Browne, a seasoned Irish journalist, asked a killer question that set off a fascinating exchange.

BROWNE: Klaus, did your taxi driver tell you how the Irish people are bewildered that we are required to pay unguaranteed bond holders billions of euros for debts that the Irish people have no relation to, or no bearing with, primarily to bail out or to ensure the sovereignty of European banks? And if your taxi driver were to ask you that question what would have been your response?

MASUCH: I would say I can understand that this is a difficult decision that was made by the government but there are a number of different issues to be balanced against each other and I understand that the government came to the view that the cost for the

Irish people, for the stability of the banking system, the confidence in the banking system, would have been much greater for the taxpayer than the action you mentioned . . . So the financial sector would have been affected, the confidence in the financial sector would have been negatively affected, and I can understand that it was a difficult decision which was taken in that direction.

BROWNE: That does not address the issue! We are required to pay on behalf of this defunct bank, in a way that has no bearing on the benefit of the Irish people at all, billions on unguaranteed bonds in order to ensure the health of the European banks. How would you explain that situation to the taxi driver that you referred to earlier?

MASUCH: I think I have addressed the question.

BROWNE: No, you have not addressed the question. You referred to the viability of the financial institutions. This institution that I am talking about is defunct. It's over. It's finished. Now, why are the Irish people required, under threat from the ECB, why are the Irish people required to pay billions to unguaranteed bond holders under the threat of the ECB?[28]

MASUCH: . . . [Inaudible]

BROWNE: You did not answer the question the last time, maybe you will answer it this time.

MASUCH: . . .

BROWNE: This is not good enough! You people are intervening in this society, causing huge damage by requiring us to make payments not for the benefit of the people here in Ireland but for the benefit of European financial institutions. You must answer the question. Why are the Irish people inflicted with this burden?

MASUCH: I think I have addressed the question . . .

BROWNE: You have nothing to say? There is no answer, is that right? Is that it? No answer?

MASUCH: I have given an answer . . .

BROWNE: You have given an answer to a different question.

MODERATOR: This is your view.

BROWNE: This is my view and it will be the view of the taxi driver!

Unable to silence the indefatigable journalist, Masuch gathered his papers and left the room with his tail between his legs. If anyone wants a visual depiction of Europe's democratic deficit or an explanation of why its citizens increasingly have no confidence in European institutions, put 'Vincent Browne versus ECB official' in your search engine, watch the clip and weep.

Through one of his characters Berthold Brecht once quipped, 'Brute force is out of date – why send out murderers when you can employ bailiffs?'[29] In the era of the troika Europe gave his quip another spin, employing

well-groomed technocrats like Mr Masuch in that capacity. Three years later, in February 2015, I was to come
face to face with Mr Masuch, he in the same role, as the
ECB's troika point man, me as the finance minister of a
Greek government elected to say no to the irrational misanthropy that passed as official European policy.[30]

As I sat opposite Klaus in a drab Brussels office,
exchanging niceties prior to beginning a tough negoti-
ation, those images from the YouTube clip featuring the
gutsy Vincent Browne came back into my mind. Our
meeting led to an impasse because, unlike the Irish government in 2009, I had authorization from my cabinet,
our parliament and the prime minister to say no to him.
Vincent Browne would have been pleased, I like to think.[31]

North and south

The Irish and the Greeks are in many ways very different
people. And yet the euro crisis merged their fortunes significantly as the weakest of the Greeks and the weakest of
the Irish were forced to cover the private losses of German and French bankers.[32]

Vincent Browne's pounding of Klaus Masuch at that
press conference put the hapless ECB official in the
impossible position of having to defend the ECB's
indefensible behaviour towards the people of Ireland. In
his questioning Browne alluded repeatedly to the ECB's
blackmail of the Dublin government, forcing it to transfer

private debts to the public purse of a bank that was dead and buried and thus posed no threat to Ireland's financial stability. Little did Browne know, however, that the ECB's dirty work was not fully done.

To begin at the beginning, when the Anglo-Irish Bank and other such financial time bombs exploded in 2009, the ECB forced the then Irish government, without the consent of its electorate, to offer the bankrupt bankers so-called promissory notes – another type of IOU – which, as every Irishman and -woman knows, bankrupted the nation, brought mass emigration back and condemned the majority to untold hardship. The promissory notes specified regular payments by the Irish treasury to the bearer of the notes that were steep and payable in a few years, thus causing both a liquidity crisis in the public sector and the insolvency of the Irish state. The defunct Irish banks took these promissory notes and deposited them as collateral with Ireland's central bank, drawing liquidity to repay their (mostly German) uninsured bond holders.

That government collapsed under the weight of its hubris, but the new Irish government bowed too to the ECB's pressure not to haircut or restructure the promissory notes. Instead Dublin adopted the 'model prisoner' strategy: 'We shall do as we are told in the hope of a later reprieve.' From then on the promissory notes sat on the books of Ireland's central bank and the Dublin government struggled to pay them as they matured. For two years the Irish government petitioned Brussels and

Frankfurt to elongate the promissory note repayment schedule while subjecting the weakest of Irish citizens to the worst cuts Northern Europe had seen since Ireland's potato famine.

Alas, the ECB was adamant: the Irish central bank was not allowed to give better terms to its own government because that would be considered a violation of the 'no bailout' clause of the Maastricht Treaty. In other words, uninsured private bankers had to be bailed out illegally[33] and utterly unethically, but the taxpayers who were forced to carry that can could not even be given better terms for repaying the odious private debt they were forced to acquire in order to bail the bankers out.

Only in 2014 did the ECB relent, accepting that the notes could be swapped for new, longer-term, interest-bearing Irish government bonds. The ECB in effect accepted that this repulsive debt should be restructured, lessening a little the strain on the Irish state. Thus Ireland's central bank swapped the hated promissory notes[34] it was holding for fresh Irish government bonds that promised their bearer significant interest payments in the long term. And, as long as the bearer was the Irish central bank, which kept these bonds to maturity, the government would pay this interest to its own central bank, which would in turn pay it back to the government as dividends. In a sense the long-term beneficiary would be Irish taxpayers, small compensation for the pain the ECB and the bankers had put them through.

But the ECB would have none of that. *What?* its Frankfurt functionaries thought. *The Irish state benefiting from the swap of the promissory notes for government bonds? We can't have that! This would be a gift to Ireland's taxpayers. Monetary financing by the* ECB *of the Irish state. What will the Bundesbank think?* And so the good people of Frankfurt pressured Ireland's central bank to unload the government bonds, to sell them to private bankers who would then, in the fullness of time, collect the interest from the Irish taxpayers. If anyone was to benefit, it ought to be the bankers and the hedge funds again. Never the citizens.

Something similar was happening at the same time in Greece. In the spring of 2012 Greece's public debt did eventually get a haircut, confirming that an unpayable debt will receive a haircut whatever the dogmas of European officials. The question was, who would lose and who would gain from the haircut's timing and features? In this case it was the bonds held mostly by Greek banks, Greek smallholders and pension funds that took a hit. The troika insisted that the Greek government do nothing to compensate the smallholders or the pension funds but that it fully reimburse the bankers.

Greek banks had indeed lost €38 billion from the haircut and were, to all intents and purposes, bankrupt.[35] So Greece's second bailout, which accompanied the haircut in the spring of 2012, set aside €50 billion that the government would borrow from the EFSF-ESM to recapitalize the banks – a sum that would, in contrast to Mario

Monti's insistence, further increase Greece's public debt. In effect, the bankrupt Greek state was forced by Europe to borrow from Europe on behalf of bankrupt Greek bankers and ensure that the latter received capital injections without losing control of their banks – without being nationalized. To allow the bankers to keep control of the banks, the Greek parliament legislated that, if the bankers showed that they could raise 10 per cent of the additional capital, the Greek state would put in the remaining 90 per cent required – the money that the taxpayer would borrow from Europe – but have no control over the running of the banks.[36]

And as if that were not enough, the same piece of legislation specified that private buyers of bank shares would receive with their shares something called warrants. Warrants are essentially options to buy more shares at the original low share price. Put differently, the state was not only allowing the bankers to remain in control of the banks they had bankrupted but was also committing itself to passing on to them whatever benefit there was from an increase in bank share prices. Heads the state lost, tails the bankers won. Simple!

Naturally, these insanely generous terms, especially the warrants, caused a whirlpool of speculative interest in Greece's banks. To seal the bankers' gains, in April 2014 a change in the bank recapitalization rules was slipped through Greece's parliament in such a manner that almost no parliamentarian noticed. An apparently innocent amendment to a bill prevented the Greek state from buying the new shares the banks were about to issue. By allowing for new shares to be issued at prices well below those that the Greek state had paid during the injection of almost €40 billion into the banks and at the same time banning the state from buying these shares, the state's shares lost value and its equity in the banks was diluted substantially. In short, the Greek public was short-changed in a way not dissimilar to what transpired in Ireland that very same week – when the Irish central bank was forced to unload the government bonds it had received for its promissory notes.

And what is the common thread between these fresh assaults on the Irish and the Greek people? The presence of Europe's custodian of the euro, the defender of the monetary realm, the pursuer of Europe's common interest: the European Central Bank.

Uneasy easing

QE was invented in Japan in the 1990s and adopted in the United States after the 2008 disaster. Once a crisis proves so large that everyone is trying, against all hope, to pay off debt in conditions of shrinking incomes, no one wants to borrow even if interest rates come down to zero. At that point central banks run out of means to stimulate the economy in their usual way – by reducing interest rates. Zero is, indeed, a radical number, and any interest rate below it means that depositors, who must now pay for the banks to hold their money, will rush to withdraw every penny, causing the banking sector's collapse.

John Maynard Keynes, back in 1936, had to quote Ibsen's *Wild Duck* in order to convey to his readers the problem that a central bank faces when interest rates fall to zero but the economy is still in the doldrums: 'The wild duck has dived down to the bottom – as deep as she can get – and bitten fast hold of the weed and tangle and all the rubbish that is down there, and it would need an extraordinarily clever dog to dive after and fish her up again.'[37] QE was meant to be Keynes's 'extraordinarily clever dog' – an alternative way by which central banks could stimulate the economy.

The idea is simple: the central bank buys from commercial banks other people's debts. Who are these 'other people'? They can be families that owe mortgages to the bank, corporations, or even a government that has sold bonds to the bank. In exchange for these debts and the stream of income they produce, the central bank deposits dollars or euros in an account the commercial bank keeps at the central bank. Where does the central bank find the money? From thin air, is the answer: they are just numbers that the central bank conjures up and adds to the commercial bank's account. Why do this? In the hope that the commercial bank will use this money by lending it to businesses wishing to invest and to families wanting to buy houses, cars, gadgets and so on. If this happens,

Where does the central bank find the money? From thin air, is the answer

economic activity will rise again as liquidity rushes in. At least this is the theory of how QE stimulates a flagging economy.

QE works but even under the best possible circumstances works neither very well nor in the manner it is intended to. The reason is that, for QE's virtuous wheel to start spinning, a multiple coincidence of impossible beliefs must occur.

Jack and Jill, who are Bank Y's customers, must trust that the property market has bottomed out in the medium term and that their jobs are secure enough to dare ask the bank for a mortgage. Bank Y must be willing to take the risk of stretching its already large assets column (list of income-generating loans) by lending Jack and Jill the money to buy a house in the hope that Bank X will buy that mortgage from it using its QE-funded reserve account at the central bank. Companies thinking of employing people like Jack and Jill in the medium to long term must believe that Bank X will indeed buy Jack and Jill's mortgage from Bank Y and, moreover, that this sort of transaction will increase demand for their products, thus justifying hiring more staff.

To cut a long story short, a great deal of believing must occur before QE delivers on its promise to boost the real economy. But given the state of self-confirming pessimism that prevails in the depths of a severe crisis, to expect that these beliefs will flood into the different agents' minds simultaneously is to believe in miracles. More likely, as we witnessed in Japan and in America, where QE was tried out with a vengeance, banks tend to lend the money conjured up by the central bank not to other banks or to Jack and Jill but to companies. Except that these companies do not invest the borrowed money in machinery and workers, fearful that the demand will not be there for extra output produced. What they do is to buy back their own shares in the stock market in order to increase their price and collect a nice bonus for having 'added value to the company'. While this process does boost, to some extent, upmarket house prices and demand for luxuries, the only genuine beneficiary is gross inequality.

In Japan and in the United States QE failed to bring about recovery[38] but at least it ensured that the recession was not allowed to turn into depression. In Europe QE was always going to prove more problematic as a result of the eurozone's shoddy architecture, reflected in the Maastricht Treaty's incongruities.

The ECB, as the Bundesbank keeps reminding Mario Draghi, does not have the right to monetize member-state debt. It cannot thus buy Italian bonds at will from Italian or Spanish banks in the way that the Fed buys treasury bills.[39] To stay as much as possible within the strictures of its charter, the Draghi-led ECB governing board came up with the following plan: bonds would be purchased from every member state in proportion to its shares in the ECB – that is, in proportion to the size of its economy. Draghi was clearly banking on the excuse that, if everyone's debt was monetized by the ECB in proportion to its economy's relative size, no one was being bailed out. Further, to counter Jens Weidmann's claim that by buying the bonds of insolvent states the ECB was edging towards buying debt from insolvent banks connected to them, Draghi accepted that nations that had fallen into the arms of the troika would have to be omitted from QE. This meant that the country with the greatest need of ECB quantitative easing, Greece, was to be excluded from it, and that the states that least needed QE, indeed economies that might be damaged by it, would get the largest dose.

The German case illustrates this well. The ECB's economists calculated that, for the ECB's eurozone-wide QE programme to work, in other words for the deflationary spiral that threatened the euro to stop, the ECB ought to purchase €60 billion worth of bonds – public debt – per month. To stick to its rulebook, the ECB was obliged to ensure that 27 per cent of these bonds were German *Bunds* (as German bonds are called), as Germany owns 27 per cent of the ECB, reflecting the fact that Germany's national income is about 27 per cent of the eurozone's aggregate national income.

The problems created by these negative interest rates were legion. German savers and pension funds, who rely on decent interest rates to survive, faced ruin. Additionally, speculators taking advantage of rock-bottom rates in Germany borrowed money to buy shares on the stock exchange, pushing the value of stocks up and thus creating financial profits for already rich Europeans at a time when working men and women were suffering low wages in Germany and devastation in places like Greece and Spain.

If Mario Draghi had been allowed to act as a properly independent central banker, he would have been able to buy only Spanish and Italian bonds, and no German *Bunds*, reflecting the fact that deflation afflicts Spain and Italy but is virtually non-existent in Germany. But no, the ECB must buy German *Bunds* in order to maintain the fiction that the ECB's silly charter is respected.

A very European coup

Mr Draghi's QE caused the price of shares and upmarket property in surplus countries like Germany and Holland to go up, but it did not help mobilize idle savings in those countries by turning them into productive investments, and it especially failed to do this in the crisis countries. And yet the financial press seems convinced that QE has worked.

In fact, what happened was that, as the quantity of euros manufactured by the ECB increased, a portion of those euros was exchanged for other currencies, and as more euros were sold in the foreign exchange markets for other currencies, the international value of the euro – its exchange rate – fell. For some countries like Spain this created a small export bonanza. But one look at Spain's devastated labour market, where wages were at rock bottom, confirms that the only jobs created by this boost were at the expense of jobs in France, where wages had not yet fallen. European corporations simply took advantage of the beleaguered Spanish, while the net effect on employment in the eurozone was negligible. The non-negligible reality is that Europe is devaluing its own labour through internal competition just as it devalued its own currencies through competition in the 1930s. In this context, Mr Draghi's QE stabilized the eurozone's deflationary forces only to allow this form of fruitless and integrity-busting beggar-thy-neighbour to take hold without actually helping to overcome the crisis.

Ironically, the greatest success of the ECB's QE policy from the perspective of Brussels, Frankfurt and Berlin was that it allowed the troika to defeat the Greek government's effort to renegotiate the failed programme that condemned our people to a never-ending depression. How did it do that?

By the end of 2012, Greece's two bailouts had completed the transfer of potential private losses onto Europe's taxpayers, thus shielding Europe's banks from the Greek drama. With the arrival of QE, the knowledge that Mr Draghi could print up to €60 or €70 billion monthly to purchase the bonds of fiscally stressed nations (except Greece's) acted as a further shock absorber in the financial markets. This allowed the Eurogroup and the

ECB to close down Greece's banks without any ensuing panic in the bond markets. A policy that was meant to curb deflation across Europe first excluded the one country that needed such treatment the most – Greece – and then strangled its newly elected government for daring to question the austerity programme and unsustainable debt that had caused the depression in the first place. Only the eurozone could have created such a despicable role for a monetary policy meant to ease its citizens' pain.

Wickedness

A few years ago, long before a political career loomed, I found myself in Brussels discussing the latest twists and turns of the crisis with one of the European Commission's high priests. It was my first discussion with anyone so high and mighty in Brussels's self-regarding technocracy, and I asked a couple of almost impertinent questions to which I was surprised to receive an honest answer.

'Why is the commission pushing Portugal to increase indirect taxes at a time of collapsing demand?' (Would such tax hikes not push sales and, by extension, the state's sales tax revenues down? So too with the doubling of taxes on heating fuel in Greece.) 'Why are you pushing for this?' I asked. 'Don't you see that people will simply not heat their homes and that government revenues from the fuel tax will fall?'

'Of course. But we are only pushing for higher sales and fuel taxes as a deterrent. The point is to demonstrate to Rome what it has coming its way if they do not comply with our demands for greater austerity there.'

More recently, when I was negotiating on the Greek government's behalf with the commission, the ECB and the IMF, I came up against exactly the same rationale. When I asked an interlocutor whether he thought that the exorbitant sales tax rates he was trying to push down my throat would improve our state's tax revenue, he freely admitted that they would not. 'So, why do you insist upon them?' I asked. His answer? 'Someone whose views matter here wants to demonstrate to Paris what is in store for France if they refuse to enact structural reforms.'

It is not therefore without justification that when I address Italian or French audiences on the subject of my recent experiences with the troika I tell them, 'I have not come here to seek your sympathy or help. I am here to warn you that there is no such thing as a Greek or Irish or Portuguese crisis. We are in it together. Greece is just a huge laboratory where failed policies are tried before being transplanted to your backyard.'

This is what the euro crisis has been doing to Europe. A clueless political elite, in denial of the nature and history of a crisis whose roots go back to at least 1971, is pursuing policies akin to carpet-bombing the economies of proud European nations in order to save them. Greece, Portugal, Ireland and Spain were beaten to a pulp in order to keep Italy and France in awe and the ECB in business. Meanwhile, these misanthropic policies are presented in the name of community, solidarity, efficiency, responsibility and, of course, heartfelt concern about the loss of the so-called credibility of European institutions.

Reverse alchemy is no easier than alchemy. The transmutation of lead into gold, the alchemist's Holy Grail, proved impossibly difficult to achieve; turning gold into lead is no easier.

Europe's reverse alchemists – the bureaucrats, politicians, commentators and academics whose accomplishments this chapter has recounted – have worked diligently and over many years to achieve something that ought to be just as impossible: the replacement of decades of continental integration with a leaden disunion that weighs heavily upon Europeans' hearts and minds. But they have achieved this – by means of a single currency.

Looking down from the heights of the famous Ferris wheel at the Prater amusement park in Vienna, Harry Lime – as played by Orson Welles in *The Third Man* – advances a provocative theory of European civilization. Under the Borgias, he says, three decades of bloodshed gave us the Renaissance. In contrast, five centuries of Swiss democracy and peaceful coexistence produced nothing more spectacular than the cuckoo clock.[40]

Facetious though Lime's theory certainly was (not to mention grossly unfair to Swiss history), European history and culture is drenched in blood and underpinned by conflict. It is the reason Europeans cherished the thought of a union. Art and music, realms in which Europe has contributed greatly to humanity, offer further evidence of our darker side. Picasso once said that a painting is not meant to decorate but to act as 'a weapon against the enemy'. Beethoven dedicated his Third Symphony to Napoleon and then tore up the dedication in anger when Napoleon declared himself an emperor. D. H. Lawrence displayed a raging contempt for democracy, with a sprinkling of virulent anti-Semitism thrown in for good measure. Ezra Pound's poetry celebrated his immense love of European culture, which alas proved no impediment to his glorification of fascism.

Against such a rich and discontented cultural background, a common currency that works to dissolve European unity seems less of a paradox. From the moment Europe was expelled from America's comforting postwar dollar zone, its elites struggled to re-create the zone within Europe. Never having grasped the lessons that the New Dealers learned during the 1930s and 1940s, European officialdom repeated the mistakes of the 1920s, creating an ill-designed currency resembling the gold standard in the heart of Europe.

From the late 1990s onwards, Europe's banks copied the practices of the Anglosphere's all-singing, all-dancing financial sector without having the safety net of a Federal Reserve, a Bank of England or even a Bank of Japan to catch them when the inevitable fall from grace occurred.

The combination of the eurozone's flimsy monetary architecture and the imperatives of Anglo-Saxon financialization, which infected the Parisian and Frankfurt banks under the noses of Brussels and the ECB, produced a reliance on money markets that Europe's monetary union could not withstand.

While the American Minotaur roared and kept German, Dutch and Chinese factories humming nicely, Europe followed Britain and the United States in subordinating its industry to finance and converting society to the new creed that markets are ends in themselves, totems to be worshipped in their own right, temples whose sanctity is beyond rational scrutiny.

There was nothing wrong with the idea of a single market from the Atlantic to Ukraine and from Shetland to Crete. Borders are scars on the planet and the sooner we dispose of them the better, as the recent Syrian refugee crisis confirms. And there is nothing wrong with a single currency either. What was dangerously wrong-headed was the idea that we could create a single market and a common currency without a powerful Demos to counterbalance, to stabilize, to civilize them.

Forget the mind-boggling economics of it all. A glance at the euro's aesthetic speaks volumes. Take a look at any euro banknote. What do you see? Pleasing arches and bridges. But these are fictitious arches and non-existent bridges. A continent replete with cultural treasures has unbelievably chosen to adorn its freshly minted common

**Borders are scars
on the planet and
the sooner we dispose
of them the better**

currency with none of them. Why? Because bureaucrats wanted nothing contentious on the new money. They wanted to remove culture from our currency in the same way they craved the depoliticization of politics and the technocratization of money. Even if one knew nothing of economics and the eurozone's hideous financial architecture, a glimpse of the cultural desert displayed on the euro notes might suffice for one to guess what would transpire. In place of a sovereign European people with a shared culture that it proudly displays on its money, Europe continued along the path of the 1950s, transferring immense political power to a colossal nominally technocratic bureaucracy that ensured democracy and solidarity were more honoured in the breach than in the observance.[41]

The Brussels-centric commentariat keeps pointing out that the demand for European Union membership has never been stronger. Is this not proof that Europe is working? They forget that the Roman empire imploded when its inner core became too brittle while its borders were expanding eastward. A cultural degeneration known as the Middle Ages was the result. Today the European Union is also seeing its core disintegrate at a time of eastward expansion. With one proud nation being subjected to fiscal waterboarding after the other; with one people turning against another, with Ponzi growth being replaced seamlessly by Ponzi austerity, with no serious discussion of how to create a rational economic architecture and with some Europeans increasingly convinced they are more deserving Europeans than others, Europe's core is weakening perilously and the bonds of authentic solidarity are breaking.

Meanwhile, across the Atlantic, the Americans are watching in disbelief as the continent they helped save from itself all those years ago is now at it again: turning against itself, sowing the seeds of conflict in its midst and in the process jeopardizing America and China's efforts to stabilize the global economy.

Is there anything that can be done to stop Europe's frightful reverse alchemy?

Can Europe snatch a democratic future from the jaws of a postmodern Dark Ages?

Or do Europeans, once again, need a helping hand from across the Atlantic, even if they do not want it?

One thing is certain: Europe is too important to be left to its clueless rulers.

Parsimony versus Austerity

THE SENTRY OUTSIDE Maximos was aghast. 'Are you going out alone, Minister?' he asked.

I nodded as the electric gate opened, mindful of the waiting photographers camped outside but determined to arrive at the Ministry of Finance on foot and in solitude. They were just as taken aback as the sentry and scrambled to follow me, laden with equipment, falling over their cables and each other. By the time I had turned left onto Queen Sophia Avenue at the corner of the National Gardens, which separate Maximos from Parliament House and Syntagma Square, they had given up.

The sun had set and a cool January breeze was rattling the remaining leaves on the trees, sending pedestrians hurrying on their way. The street lights had not yet come on, and in the dusk it took a few moments to locate the tree, enshrined with flowers and handwritten messages, next to which Dimitris Christoulas, the retired pharmacist, had shot himself. With almost no one around, I took a moment to build a mental bridge between that tree and the brightly lit offices of the Ministry of Finance that I could see opposite. A moment later I had crossed Philhellenes Street to enter the ministry that would be my crucible for the next 162 days. As I entered the building, a cheer rose from the fifty or so women camped outside: some of the ministry's legendary cleaners, who had been dismissed overnight and without compensation two years before by the previous government. 'Don't betray us!' they shouted.

'I won't,' I replied firmly as I headed for the lift.

The lift door opened onto the sixth floor, and a secretary led me to the ministerial suite where my predecessor awaited. He was alone and greeted me graciously. His desk was strikingly bare. None of the gadgets that fill a modern office was in sight, not even a computer. Its only visible weapon against the sea of troubles that besieged it was an icon of the Madonna on the shelf behind the minister's desk. The large high-backed desk chair, which was no doubt intended to project authority, looked as uncomfortable as it was ugly. The array of old-fashioned phones on a side desk were straight out of a 1970s movie, and the books on the shelf were clearly gifts that no previous minister had cared enough to read or take away. The oil paintings on the wall were on loan from the National Gallery. It would have taken only a word to have them replaced, but I felt no urge to get comfortable in that office.

The rest of the furniture had an air of decadence, especially the fading red velvet couch – perfect, I thought, for the finance ministry of a bankrupt state. The only exception was a large rectangular wooden meeting table, which I immediately decided would become my workstation, a long way from the ministerial desk, which I made a point of never using. The table made me feel as at home as it was possible or desirable to feel in that spacious but sad office with such a sorry recent past. The office had one outstanding redeeming feature: a wide, tall window offering a magnificent view of Syntagma Square and Parliament House beyond. One look through it is enough to stiffen the resolve of anyone who has ever harboured an ounce of pride in modern Greece's long struggle for democracy.

My predecessor was gentle, pleasant and visibly relieved that his ordeal was over. He had two dossiers for me, one medium-sized blue one and a bulging red file. The blue dossier contained ministerial decrees that he had not had the opportunity to sign and which he encouraged me to consider. The red dossier was labelled 'FACTA' and pertained to a deal that the United States was ultra-keen to foist onto every country, which would allow the US Treasury to keep tabs on American citizens' foreign financial transactions.[1] Intriguingly, he had no documents to hand over regarding Greece's loan agreement with the EU and the IMF, though he offered to brief me on our repayment schedule, which of course I could already recite, chapter and verse. Days later, when I asked for a copy of the original second bailout loan agreement, I received the astounding reply: 'Minister, your predecessor seems to have taken the only copy with him, along with his private archive.' Curious as this may sound, it was not the most stupefying discovery of those early days.

While I would have enjoyed the chance to discuss with him his failed last-ditch attempt to conclude the second bailout programme, which was meant to have ended three weeks before, the discussion would have been of academic interest only – concluding the bailout was impossible for the simple reason that it had been designed at the outset to fail.[2] Meanwhile, most of the country's news journalists, a forest of cameras, foreign correspondents and various curious officials had assembled in the ministry's press room, awaiting the traditional press conference held jointly by the outgoing and incoming ministers, and were becoming increasingly restless. We had to move on.

Before we did, my predecessor asked me to give some thought to keeping three of his non-permanent staff, especially a single mother who would have faced intolerable hardship were I to let her go. Naturally, I agreed. At the same time I suddenly realized that the three secretaries in the minister's office whom I had just met were not civil servants but his private employees. As such, they would be leaving too. After the press conference I would return to an empty sixth floor to engage in battle with the world's most powerful creditors without secretaries, staff or indeed a computer. Thankfully, I had my trusty laptop in my rucksack. But who would furnish me with the Wi-Fi password?

After a dignified speech by the outgoing minister, it was my chance to set the scene. 'The state must have continuity,' I said after thanking my predecessor for his efforts. 'But there will be no continuity of the motivated error that began to devastate our society in 2010 and which has been repeated continuously ever since: treating our state's insolvency as a shortage of liquidity.'

Once I had outlined my analysis of how Greece's impossible debt and unacknowledged bankruptcy had caused the depression, I turned to a distinction of great importance, one that left-wingers and Keynesians often fail to highlight: that between parsimony and austerity. 'We are in favour of parsimony,' I said, surprising many in the audience.

> Greeks did splendidly when we lived austere lives, when we spent less than we earned, when we channelled our savings to the education of our children, when we were proud that we were not in debt . . . But an austere life is one thing and Ponzi austerity is quite another. Over the past years we have had a phoney austerity that cuts the low incomes of the weak while adding mountains of new debt to existing mountain ranges of unpayable debt. We shall end this practice, beginning at home, within this ministry, where parsimony will edge austerity out.

With huge reductions in private expenditure and massive cuts in public spending, families and companies were unable to make ends meet. In other words, the government's attempt to create an unfeasible public surplus had made it impossible for people to live within their means. Put simply, public austerity had to end because it was killing private parsimony. We would begin with the Ministry of Finance's own accounts. To demonstrate the principle, I announced a symbolic move: the immediate sale of the two BMW 7 series armour-plated limousines that a previous minister had ordered for himself, costing a scandalous €750,000, I was informed. My motorcycle would do nicely, especially in the infuriating Athens traffic. I also announced that I and my two deputy ministers would desist from hiring the hordes of expensive advisers which had invaded the ministry with each previous administration, not to mention the multinational consultancy companies that charged tens of millions to deliver catastrophic advice. Parsimony would thus return to the Ministry of Finance under a new administration whose main aim was to put an end to austerity.

When a few days later I travelled to Brussels and Berlin to begin talks with officials, one of the first things they took issue with was another of the announcements I had made in that first press conference: the rehiring of the three hundred cleaners who had been sacked by the previous government, some of whom had cheered me as I entered the ministry. 'Backtracking on reforms' was the expression used to criticize me. Some even suggested that rehiring the cleaners was a *casus belli*. The fact that I had saved many times their wages through genuine parsimony did not matter to them, nor did the perverse morality of casually paying tens of millions of euros for a few days' worth of calamitous advice while dismissing the people who cleaned up after the consultants for no more than €400 a month. (The fact that standards of hygiene had declined was apparently also considered immaterial.) If the country's bankruptcy was to be blamed on its victims, then the ministry's cleaners were ideal scapegoats.

But the cleaners' gender and class, their demonstrable powerlessness, their dependence on the state for a minimally safe job, their defiance and determination to camp outside the Ministry of Finance for months on end were to my mind symbolic of something else. They reminded me of the British women who had set up a peace camp in 1981 at Greenham Common to protest against the deployment of new medium-range US nuclear missiles. Those women drew upon themselves the ire, eventually the hatred, of an establishment that recognized in them a challenge to its patriarchal authority. So it was with the ministry's cleaning women: not only did they symbolize the groundswell of public feeling against austerity, they threatened to feminize the struggle, just as women partisans had against the Nazi occupation of the 1940s.

At any rate, their dismissal, literal and metaphorical, exemplified the policy of victimizing the depression's victims in order to teach the Greek citizenry that it was to blame for the nation's implosion. By sacking them, the previous government was demonstrating the cleaners' guilt. By rehiring them I was committing a sin worse even than championing parsimony at the expense of austerity.

Moderation versus subservience

As I saw it, my task as the finance minister of a bankrupt country was not to offer false hope through fake optimism, but rather to promote moderate policies and realistic expectations. So I was pleased to be able to conclude that first press conference with a genuinely good piece of news with regard to our impending negotiations.

'TV evangelists of subservience have been calling upon us for weeks now to issue a declaration of allegiance to the troika and its programme, for otherwise Europe will not even talk to us,' I said. 'Anyone calling for this must have a poor opinion of Europe.' I then went on to describe a telephone conversation I had had on election day with Jeroen Dijsselbloem, president of the Eurogroup and finance minister of the Netherlands.

Jeroen had called to congratulate me on our victory and lost no time before asking the obvious question: what were our intentions regarding the ongoing Greek programme? I replied as accommodatingly as possible while making the point that had to be made: our new government, I said, recognized that it had inherited certain commitments to the Eurogroup while hoping and trusting that its partners would also recognize that we had been elected to renegotiate key elements of our loan agreement and its associated programme. Thus it was incumbent upon us all to find common ground – a bridge I called it – between the existing programme and the new government's priorities and views. Jeroen agreed immediately with a plain, 'This is very good,' proposing to pay me a visit on the following Friday, 30 January 2015. Out of courtesy I offered to visit him in Brussels instead if that suited him better, but he insisted that he and his entourage should honour their new Greek colleagues with a visit.

Encouraged by Jeroen's acceptance of our common task – to throw a solid bridge over the chasm between their programme and our mandate – and with an eye to the unfolding bank run that the previous regime and the Bank of Greece had fuelled weeks before, I emphasized my determination to establish common ground. As for the narrative of confrontation that the media were perpetuating, I went to some lengths to dispel it at the press conference:

> Journalists like to report on conflict. They see *High Noon* shootouts everywhere. I was listening to the BBC portray my impending meeting with Jeroen Dijsselbloem as a shootout, as a game of chicken to see who will blink first. I understand the appeal of such depictions to

ratings-hungry journalism. But Jeroen and I agreed that we shall deconstruct the foundation upon which predictions of belligerent clashes are based. There will be no threats. It is not a matter of who will yield first. The euro crisis only has victims. The only winners are the bigots, the racists, those who invest in fear and division and in the serpent's egg, as Ingmar Bergman might have said.[3] With Jeroen Dijsselbloem on Friday we shall build on a relationship that annuls Europe's deconstruction.

I meant every single word.

After the press conference I returned to the offices on the sixth floor to find them eerily empty. My predecessor had left, along with his staff, leaving behind two young women almost trembling in expectation of being instantly dismissed by their new 'radical Left' boss. I reassured them that the last thing I had time for was a purge of the previous regime's staff, closed the door behind me and pulled up a chair at the large table. I took my laptop out of my rucksack, plugged it into the mains and, while waiting for it to boot up, looked out of the window that framed Parliament House, my mind racing to compile a list of the day's most pressing priorities.

When I looked back to my laptop screen, I remembered that I did not have the Wi-Fi password. I got up, opened the door to the secretaries' office and called out, 'Anyone here?'

Soon one of the two visibly relieved and somewhat

embarrassed secretaries appeared from some distant room. Half an hour later we located someone who knew someone else who knew the password. And thus the new minister acquired a very, very slow connection to the Internet – not the most auspicious beginning to a long, lonely campaign against the most highly weaponized and best prepared creditors in the history of capitalism.

Back to the Future

EVERY TIME I sat on the ministerial benches in Greece's parliament, immediately opposite me sat the democratically elected thugs of the Nazi party Golden Dawn.[1] Each time I failed to avoid their gaze, or when friends from the United States, Britain, Australia, Thailand or China asked me to explain the Golden Dawn phenomenon, I was reminded of the figure of Kapnias.

The first time I met Kapnias was in December 1991, at the southern Peloponnese farm he shared with Grandma Georgia, his wife, whom I was visiting and whose life story deserves to be the centrepiece of some talented tragedian's labour of love.[2] Having driven from Athens to spend a weekend with them, I caught my first glimpse of him standing next to his goats, a hawk hovering motionless overhead against the backdrop of an electric-blue sky. A dishevelled yet not undistinguished figure dressed in the work clothes poor Mediterranean farmers think of as their uniform, his octogenarian weather-beaten face, covered in white stubble, smiled at me. A friendly and at once ominous smile packed with the promise of disturbing yarns and indecipherable truths. 'We meet at last! Welcome to my humble abode,' he cried, spreading his arms.

Although Kapnias's reputation had preceded him, I was not prepared for the quiet ferocity of that night's welcome. After settling into the bedroom that Grandma Georgia had adoringly prepared and having broken bread with them, I excused myself and drove to the nearby town to meet local friends. Upon returning to the farmhouse, well after midnight, I could hear Kapnias's distant snoring and an array of excited cats. Exhausted, I was ready for a night's rest in the lap of the Peloponnese countryside. Then I saw the two books resting on my pillow.

One was entitled *Memoirs of a Prime Minister*. Its author was Adamantios Androutsopoulos, the last prime minister of the military dictatorship that had darkened my youth and the puppet of Dimitrios Ioannidis, the brigadier who took the neo-fascist junta further into neo-Nazi territory after the student massacre of 17 November 1973. The second book was a small leather-bound volume in an advanced state of disrepair. Incredulous even after I had read the title, *Mein Kampf*, I opened it. It was an original German edition, published somewhere in Germany in 1934. Bedtime material to shock the visiting leftie with, I surmised. Courtesy of a semi-illiterate farmer who clearly wanted to make a point.

Upon waking in the morning, I took my time getting out of bed, hoping that Kapnias had headed out to tend to his animals and crops in the meantime. To no avail. He was never going to miss my emergence, overflowing with eagerness to gauge my reaction to his late-night offerings. And so we started talking.

Kapnias was once an 'untouchable' farmhand bonded to Grandma Georgia's father, who before the war was something of a nobleman in the mountainous village of their origin – a beautiful village that was virtually depopulated by the 1944–9 civil war. During the Nazi occupation (1941–4) Georgia's father liaised between British intelligence and the local left-wing partisans, sabotaging in unison the nearby *Wehrmacht* brigade and several platoons of Italian soldiers. Georgia, the local beauty, fell in love and secretly married George Xenos, one of the partisans. Against the background of a harsh war, two young children were born to the defiantly happy couple.

Meanwhile, Kapnias, the teenage menial, decided to throw his lot in with the other side: he joined a paramilitary unit assembled by the local Gestapo and was sent to Crete for training in the art of interrogation and countersubversion. It was there that Hans, his instructor, gave him the leather-bound copy of *Mein Kampf*, like those preachers who hand out copies of the Bible to illiterate natives before moving on to proselytize others.

The Second World War ended, but the conflict in Greece intensified as the country sank into the mire of a nightmarish civil war. Allies turned against one another, brother against brother, daughter against father. Xenos, Georgia's partisan husband, found himself fighting the national army put together by the British of which her father was a local stalwart. Within two years a modern Greek tragedy had unfolded. Xenos was injured in battle against the national army and finished off by an American officer during the interrogation that followed his capture.[3] Georgia's father was killed soon after by her husband's partisan comrades for having also finished off an injured partisan who had sought refuge in his home. Thus Georgia was widowed by her father's nationalists and orphaned by her husband's partisans.

These events were Kapnias's cue. Having made the transition from Gestapo-organized paramilitary to local gendarmerie, he was now in a position to exact revenge on the upper class of his small quasi-feudal universe. He approached Georgia with a proposal: 'You marry me, and I shall stop my ilk from ridding the land of you and your communist seed,' referring to her two young orphans. Georgia acquiesced, hoping that Kapnias's uniform would provide safety for herself and her children, whose origins she shrouded in the convenient lie that their partisan father had been murdered by the partisans. Alas, not long after their bleak wedding, Kapnias was dismissed from the gendarmes for using excessive force during an interrogation – a little like being fired by Mephistopheles for excessive malice. His wrath and associated brutality then turned against his new wife, her seed and the whole world. Thus Georgia bought her family's survival at the price of a life of abuse, poverty, tears and terror under Kapnias's permanently cruel regime. She was never to find respite until her death in 2012.

Back then I had assumed that figures like Kapnias were a dying breed whose like would fade from the land of our parents. It was not to be, as the sight of the Golden Dawn deputies in the Athens Parliament House confirmed some years later.

Serpent DNA

Nothing prepares a people for authoritarianism better than defeat followed closely by national humiliation and an economic implosion.[4] Germany's defeat in the Great War and its submission to the Versailles Treaty, coupled with the middle class's economic calamity a little later, played a well-documented role in the rise of the Nazis. Greece suffered a comparable defeat and humiliation in 1922 at the hands of Mustafa Kemal as a result of its own government's hubris.[5] The political instability that followed this military and economic catastrophe, coupled with the intensification of poverty after the 1929 global crisis, gave rise to our own variety of fascism, the regime of Ioannis Metaxas installed by a coup on 4 August 1936.

Of course none of this was out of the ordinary. Only a

few days before Greece's fascist regime was born, Spain was falling into the same crevasse with Generalissimo Franco's assault on the Republicans. Italy had turned to fascism ten years earlier under Mussolini, as had Portugal under Salazar. Hungary, Serbia, Romania, Bulgaria and the Baltic states all fell to some variant of the serpent.[6] Even Britain had its brush with Oswald Mosley's black-shirts, not to mention several royals of a pro-Nazi disposition. Today we tend to forget that the spectre of fascism haunted most of Europe well before Hitler's first cannon shots, air raids and Panzer divisions kick-started the Second World War.

We also forget that the dream of European union pre-dated the war. The spirit of Charlemagne, which French president Valéry Giscard d'Estaing and Chancellor Helmut Schmidt invoked decades later in support of Europe's monetary union, had a sordid history of earlier invocations. In late 1944, when it was evident to all with eyes to see and ears to hear that Hitler had lost the war, between seven and eleven thousand Frenchmen enlisted in a new SS division named after Charlemagne – to give it its full name, the 33rd Waffen Grenadier Division of the SS Charlemagne (1st French). In the months that followed they fought doggedly and were the last SS unit to defend the Führer's bunker, fighting to the bitter end.[7] Something motivated those Frenchmen to fight, and that something had to do with the idea of a *Paneuropa* worthy of Charlemagne's legacy, which Hitler represented in their deluded minds. This is a potent reminder that the symbols of European unity, having fallen prey to our continent's dark side once, may easily do so again.

Today Europeans assume that our continent's dark side has been eradicated. That the European Economic Community, which evolved with the Maastricht Treaty of 1993 into the European Union, constitutes a bulwark against totalitarianism. While it is true that after the war Europeans imagined the continent's new European institutions were defences against another war and another totalitarianism, it is not at all evident that the actual institutions we created were entirely consistent with this aspiration. If a grasp of history is a prerequisite for averting the resurrection of various forms of evil, this assumption must be interrogated. The task below may help in doing so.

Take a look at the following two quotations and guess who, and in what context, might have uttered such stirring words.

> Above and beyond the concept of the nation state, the idea of a new community will transform the living space given us all by history into a new spiritual realm . . . The new Europe of solidarity and cooperation among all its peoples, a Europe without unemployment, without monetary crises . . . will find an assured foundation and rapidly increasing prosperity once national economic barriers are removed.

The symbols of European unity, having fallen prey to our continent's dark side once, may easily do so again

The people of Europe understand increasingly that the great issues dividing us, when compared with those which will emerge and will be resolved between continents, are nothing but trivial family feuds . . . I am convinced that in fifty years Europeans will not be thinking in terms of separate countries.

The first of the two speakers was Arthur Seyss-Inquart, a Nazi who, as Austria's newly appointed chancellor, signed the Anschluss before becoming minister of security and the interior in the post-Anschluss Nazi government. Later he was anointed prefect of occupied Holland. In the quote above he was addressing his Dutch subjects in 1940.[8] Seyss-Inquart was sentenced to death at the Nuremberg trials in 1946. The second is Joseph Goebbels, speaking in 1940.[9]

Does the fact that the Nazis were the first to plan a European economic and monetary union – one perhaps too close for comfort to today's European Union – imply that the latter was founded on fascist principles? No, of course it does not. The important point is not that the European Union was spawned by the serpent but, rather more constructively, that Europeans have a moral duty to dispel the dangerous illusion that the notion of a European union within which nationalisms and the nation state are supposed gradually to dissolve is inherently incompatible with the autocratic, misanthropic, racist, inhuman warmongers who rose to prominence as a result of the interwar European crisis. However, a united Europe based on free trade, free capital movements, common labour laws and a single currency is unfortunately as compatible with a Nazi agenda as it is with a progressive, humanist, internationalist one. A sobering thought which Europe today has an obligation to keep in its collective mind.

Conferences on European integration, common agricultural policies, coordinated industrial policies, joint schemes to promote technological progress, monetary union and so on are not in themselves moves in the direction of a brighter European future. The first such conference, with the full participation of academics, government ministers and officials, to discuss (and I quote from the official programme) 'the formation of a European Economic Community' took place in Berlin in 1942 under the auspices of Walther Funk, Hitler's finance minister. What this means is that a European union very much like the one now administered by the Brussels technocracy is not incompatible with totalitarianism.

A multitude of evils can hide behind the ideological veil of top-down European integration, especially when it is accomplished in the midst of (even by means of) a vicious asymmetrical recession. Europeanists craving to imagine Europe as our common home, but who also sensibly fear that Europe is sliding into authoritarianism, threatening to turn our common home into a shared concentration camp, better beware. The slide into totalitarianism is not to be prevented by technical means applied by faceless bureaucrats primarily concerned with their own banal careers. It can be prevented only by a functioning, healthy democracy. By precisely the political process that Brussels and Frankfurt officials disdain so deeply and which every twist of the troika's screw depletes. With every toxic bailout, with each triumph of the Eurogroup over a democratically elected government, Europe is pushed further into a dark and arid future consistent with the serpent's plans.

The evidence is all around us. Today, as of this writing, France's National Front, with its roots deeply buried in a racist Holocaust-denying mythology, is predicted to top the first round of the next presidential election. Hungary has a government with ultra-right-wing credentials. In the Baltics memorial services commemorating local Nazis who joined the SS and fought alongside the Charlemagne Division are held frequently, often attended by democratically elected government ministers. Political parties and paramilitary groups with allegiances to the memory of the Nazis' wartime collaborators remain influential in Ukraine, Serbia, Croatia and Albania.

Be that as it may, Greece remains a puzzling outlier. Only in my home country did an unashamedly Nazi party, Golden Dawn, manage to register impressive electoral results. Why are the Nazis back in Greece's parliament? The Spaniards, the Irish, the Portuguese and the Italians have also felt the impact of the eurozone crisis in their bones. So why is it that only Greece has an out-and-out Nazi party in parliament with its storm troopers terrorizing the streets?

The main reason is that the economic collapse in Greece was far more serious than those which took place in the other eurozone countries. Having fallen first, after the 2008 global crash, Greece became the troika's laboratory. The most unsustainable public debt was dealt with by means of the largest bailout loans accompanied by the harshest austerity. The experiment failed disastrously, with almost a third of all incomes and jobs lost and debt casting an increasingly long shadow over Greece within which nothing flourishes but fear and loathing. So, when it turned its attention to the other failed eurozone member states, the troika was already fearful of the zone's survival. To make some amends for the wasteland it had created in Greece, it applied much lighter versions of austerity to Ireland, Portugal, Spain and Italy. Less austerity, shallower recessions, less room for Nazism to grow roots.

Another reason for the re-emergence of fascism in Greece is hidden in Kapnias's story. In Greece the occupying Nazis attempted to create a local SS-like body of marginalized men disaffected with both the local bourgeoisie and the Left and living under a permanent cloud of collective disgrace brought on by a previous national humiliation. 'Kapnias' was a nickname (his real name was George) derived from the Greek words for tobacco (*kapnos*) and for soot (*kapnia*), words whose destructive bitterness Kapnias embraced as representative of his image: a bitter, angry man perpetually seeking revenge on a world that had never given him a chance. Until, that is, the Gestapo offered him one; a chance that he grabbed with both hands and which he savoured to the bitter end, surrounded by his innocent, unsuspecting goats.

During our long conversations Kapnias appeared intoxicated with the power that his Nazi instructors had given him. Attuned to his own empowerment from an alliance with the dark side, he revelled in the retreat from decency that was to mark his life thereafter. 'The Germans were above God,' he told me. 'Unlike the Italians or our own mob, they could use any means to get the job done. Without wincing! With no fear! No passion! . . . You had to see them with your own eyes.' 'They were magnificent' was his last utterance on the matter, his face lighting up like a Christmas tree, his heart filled with extra pleasure from noticing that my stomach was turning with every one of his words.

And yet I understood where he was coming from. Being handed that little leather-bound book, which Kapnias did not have the German to read, was for him like induction into a European brotherhood – an evil one, undoubtedly, but one that was also vastly more technologically advanced than his own community, giving a marginalized cowardly man like Kapnias a priceless sense of belonging to some circle of the select. A sense that can elicit a hideous outpouring of violent sentiments, words, acts.

The influence of Kapnias-like misanthropes faded but did not die out after the left-wing partisans were crushed in 1949. Men of his ilk higher up in the state's hierarchy remained central to the postwar Greek state, murdering left-wing parliamentarian Grigoris Lambrakis in 1963,[10] taking power in 1967 with a military coup and remaining present in various state institutions after that regime's collapse in 1974.

Kapnias died in 2009, as did around that period most of his wartime brethren. However, the serpent's DNA did not perish with them; it remained dormant, awaiting the next crisis to sprout again.

Migrant dreams, Ponzi growth, mounting discontent

When Greece managed to enter the eurozone in 2001, it was largely due to the influx into the country of migrant labour in the 1990s from across the collapsed Iron Curtain. Spain and Italy also benefited greatly from undocumented foreign workers, who boosted their competitiveness indices and helped them put on a display of convergence towards the Maastricht criteria. But while Europe's periphery, from Greece to Iberia and from there to Ireland, was abuzz with the sound of bulldozers and drills funded by stressed bankers like my travelling companion Franz, the gigantic struggle to get these countries into the eurozone had in fact condemned a large segment of their poorer citizens to a slow-burning unseen recession.

Economic activity was booming but, beneath the surface, good jobs were disappearing: while most investment in the periphery was being pumped into building bubbles, traditional manufacturing centres were actually dying out, drowned by waves of manufactures imported from the more advanced surplus economies. Bubbles offer great opportunities for spivs but create very little meaningful, sustainable employment, especially when large German, Dutch and French conglomerates rush in to purchase local firms, wind down their manufacturing activities and use their premises as warehouses to stock goods imported from their own plants.[11] Boom times in Europe's periphery coincided paradoxically with falling living standards for the weak. Even as they bought new cars and refrigerators on credit, they knew the tide of liquidity might one day turn into torrents of liquidations.

True, wages rose during the eurozone's golden decade, from 1998, when official interest rates were equalized, to 2008. In some cases, such as in Greece, Ireland, France and Spain, we were told that they were rising too fast, making these economies less competitive in relation to Germany, Finland, Holland and the rest, where labour costs per unit of output were either falling or rising more slowly. And yet discontent was rising too. In Germany the reason was obvious: workers worked harder, their companies were generating unprecedented profits, but wages weren't keeping up and their living standards were stagnant. But why was there even more discontent in countries such as France, Spain and Greece, when official statistics, television presenters, newspaper reports and politicians were telling us that we had never had it so good, that our purchasing power was on the rise, that prosperity was engulfing us?

A close look at the official statistics suffices to dispel the superficial paradox. Wages were indeed rising in the deficit nations a little faster than the average speed with which prices grew, so it was true that the 'average' Greek, Irish person, Spaniard was indeed doing better. Except that there is no such thing as an average Greek, Irish person or Spaniard. In fact, the prices of basic goods – the things that everyone must buy, however poor – were actually rising much faster than average. Meanwhile, the prices of luxury goods, such as those purchased by the top 10 per cent, were falling dramatically.[12] On average, wages were rising, except that the majority of working people were doing far worse than average – not least because that average was heavily skewed by the huge salaries of the oligarchs' managers and by falling prices for goods that only privileged folk could afford.[13]

Alongside this burgeoning division between rich and poor, another insidious fault line was growing: between native workers and migrant workers. The latter were more mobile, willing to suffer humiliations that locals would reject, and therefore willing to work for less and take advantage of jobs in places that natives, wedded to immobile families and heavy housing costs, could not move to. The weak were thus getting weaker, divided and discontented, while the strong grew more affluent and cockier than ever. And all this during the largest Ponzi growth scheme in history, during which Spain was inundated with white elephants such as motorways to nowhere, Greece became one huge construction site, spewing out highways, metro systems and the 2004 Olympic venues, and the Celtic Tiger was either building endless rows of apartment blocks in the middle of nowhere or littering Dublin's skyline with commercial 'spaces'.

Concealed by the cacophony of so much moneymaking, the serpent's egg was incubating nicely, kept warm by a hidden recession felt only by the weak and unacknowledged by the champagne-popping commentariat; blue-collar workers were increasingly abandoned to the sirens of racist misanthropy. With Europe's Left nursing its wounds from the historic defeat of 1991, when the Soviet empire collapsed, and with social democratic parties scrambling to jump on financialization's bandwagon, the only political parties that fed on the growing discontent were racist, ultra-nationalist organizations like France's National Front, Italy's Northern League and of course Greece's Golden Dawn.

By 2005 the rate at which Wall Street, the City of London and Frankfurt's banks were minting private money had slowed a little. That minor reduction in the rate of

Ponzi growth made it harder for paperless migrant workers to find jobs. To offer an example, as the 2004 Olympics in Athens drew closer, the migrants who had been labouring like ants to get the stadia ready in time for the athletes and dignitaries suddenly had no jobs. They became more visible but simultaneously less lucrative. Not only were they 'bloody foreigners', they now had less money to spend too. Similarly, in France and elsewhere throughout Europe the serpent's hatchlings were ready to break from their shells, blaming the immigrants for the hidden recession afflicting weaker locals actually caused by the eurozone's inherent design faults.

France's electoral map showed a stark shift in votes from left-wing parties traditionally associated with defending the weak to the National Front; socialist president Mitterrand's chickens were coming home to roost. So too in Greece, Italy, Ireland and Spain, where centre-left parties, having played a central role in bringing about monetary union, had now lost moral authority and saw many of their voters turning to the intransigent, nationalist Right.

Around the same time Greece's Nazis shifted up a gear, planning a campaign of 'cleansing' neighbourhoods that brought despair to survivors of the 1930s. Copying a strategy pioneered by the German ultra-rightist National Democratic Party in eastern Germany in the 1990s, Golden Dawn aimed at 'liberating' the suburbs in which many of the migrants lived. They called them 'brown scum' and soon set up 'citizens' committees' which were effectively supremacist vigilante groups, tolerated and in many cases aided by the police.[14]

Before long certain areas like Attiki Square (not far from the centre of Athens) became dangerous for anyone who dared look different. Migrant-owned shops were repeatedly targeted Kristallnacht-style, and the victims learned the hard way that it was pointless to take the matter to the police. Property developers saw in Golden Dawn a nice little earner – buy properties at low prices, have the migrants removed forcibly by Golden Dawn and then cash in. Even mainstream television stations gave a platform to 'incensed locals' describing migrants as rabies-infected animals that had to be quarantined, if not put down. Before long, the list of those who had it coming included prostitutes, gays, lesbians, transsexuals and, of course, left-wing migrant lovers.

Then came the American Minotaur's demise and the subsequent economic tsunami that bankrupted Greece in late 2009 and led to the so-called bailout of May 2010. The steel strings of austerity that accompanied the massive loan agreement then demolished Greece's social economy. With Golden Dawn in place and the political centre going down the drain along with the country's economy, a Nazi revival was on the cards. The figure of Kapnias suddenly turned from a reminder of a terrible past to a very contemporary presence.

While Greece is an outlier, and the swastika is not

being waved by crowds in the rest of Europe, racism and the whiff of evil are spreading throughout the continent. This was made hideously apparent during the summer of 2015, when the leaders of supposedly civilized European countries seemed to compete with each other as to who would offer sanctuary to the fewest refugees arriving from war-torn Syria. But this should not surprise us. While the unimpeded movement of goods, money and moneyed executives has always been a sacred cow of globalized finance and the founding principle of free trade zones such as the European Union, the North American Free Trade Agreement or the Transatlantic Trade and Investment Partnership, the equivalent freedom of movement for ordinary people has always been severely circumscribed. No wonder then that racism grows in proportion to our free trade zones' economic crises.

Nazis in power, even though not in government

Many will rightly point out the great differences between Europe now and the Europe of the 1930s: for example, today no Nazi party is close to taking control of a government in Europe. However, ultra-rightist movements do not need to be in government in order to be in power. Not only has France's National Front legitimized an openly xenophobic nationalist narrative, it has heavily influenced the policies of mainstream parties: a large part of France's political spectrum has shifted rightward in a reactive move to prevent the loss of more formerly left-leaning working-class votes to them.

Greece's Golden Dawn got its first taste of real power just *before* the election of May 2012, when it would score its first electoral success. It came in the form of a despicable decree issued by the then minister of public order, Michalis Chrysohoidis, a long-time socialist party minister. Chrysohoidis and his colleague Andreas Loverdos, then minister of health, mounted a campaign against the weakest women in Greece. Loverdos even addressed a United Nations conference, informing his flabbergasted audience that Greek 'family men' were being put at risk by HIV-infected African prostitutes.[15] The two ministers ordered the police to arrest prostitutes in central Athens, many of them undocumented migrants, forcibly subject them to HIV tests and post their photographs and names on the ministry's website so as to warn potential Greek clients.

Over several weeks the police swept central Athens, arresting with no warrant any woman who did not seem to them sufficiently respectable, shoving her in a van and taking her to a police station, where officers restrained her while a blood sample was extracted. If the HIV test came back positive, they would throw the hapless woman into a police cell without any counselling whatsoever, charged with endangering public health. In one fell swoop, a swathe of liberal democracy's cherished principles were torn up. For what? So that two embattled socialist politicians could profit electorally from a moral panic based on xenophobic narratives that were grist to the mill of organizations like Golden Dawn.[16]

It is in this sense that Golden Dawn found itself in power even before it entered parliament. Why should its thugs care about being elected if its policies were being implemented by mainstream politicians occupying ministries under the command of the troika of Greece's lenders? True ideologues, the Golden Dawn brutes celebrated the conversion of their sinister agenda into Bailoutistan's public policy.

A few weeks later, in June 2012, two consecutive elections delivered a new Greek government under the leadership of conservative Antonis Samaras. The government lost no time in passing an extraordinary piece of legislation clarifying that Greek citizenship and good grades in college entrance examinations were not sufficient for a young person to enter Greece's police or military academies. What else was needed? Proof of *ithageneia* – Greek blood lineage – which naturalized migrants of course lacked. Why? To play to Golden Dawn voters, who like all fascists have a penchant for blood and land, hoping to entice them back to the fold of the right-wing mainstream.

Thus, for the first time since the Nazi laws of the 1930s, a European country introduced legislation that classified its citizens (not just its residents) according to who had the 'right blood' and who didn't. A terrifying chill ought to travel through our spines at the very thought, and a deep shame ought to fill our hearts that this should be allowed to occur in the world today.

Lotus eaters

One hot June afternoon in 1968, a little more than a year after the colonels had come to power and cast a shadow over our lives, my mother and I were walking just outside the ancient stadium where the first modern-era Olympics had been staged in 1896. A newsboy announced at the top of his voice that someone called Bobby Kennedy was dead. My mother's eyes filled with tears. I vividly recall her first words after regaining her composure: 'He was our last chance.'

In my childhood two German-speaking politicians and an American featured as figures of hope. The chancellors of Germany and Austria, Willy Brandt and Bruno Kreisky, were social democrats who had stood up to Greek fascism and created pockets of authentic solidarity in which we could take shelter. The American was Senator Bobby Kennedy, the renowned champion of the Civil Rights Movement and in 1968 a popular Democrat candidate for the presidency. To my mother, Bobby Kennedy represented hope that the United States would regret their support for our neo-fascist dictators and facilitate a return to democratic rule. Her grief at the news of his murder was motivated by her despair that a powerful defender of the weak had been lost.

With hindsight, Bobby Kennedy represented something else too: perhaps the last American who could have kept the spirit of the New Deal alive in the White House. With his death and with Lyndon Baines Johnson gone from the scene, there was no one to stand in the way of the Nixon Shock which would irreversibly unleash forces that unhinged Europe.

Once upon a time, Europe's social democrats and American New Dealers understood what their role ought to be. They knew that civilizing capitalism required the deployment of a portion of the industrialists' profits to fund projects such as hospitals, schools, unemployment insurance and the arts. Bruno Kreisky, Willy Brandt, Swedish social democrat Olof Palme,[17] Britain's Labour Party all understood that this was their task. Some were more successful than others but they all shared that same basic conviction. But when financialization rode into town on the Minotaur's back, some time after 1980, all this changed.

In the 1980s and 1990s Europe's social democrats and America's Democrats abandoned the idea that capitalism had to be civilized by driving a hard bargain with the captains of industry, supporting organized labour and containing the bankers' natural instincts. They forgot that unregulated labour and financial and property markets are profoundly inefficient. They ignored inequality created as a by-product of that inefficiency. They lost sight of the fact that inequality destabilizes financial markets and reinforces capitalism's tendency to fall on its face.

What possessed the Clinton administration to dismantle the New Deal's last remaining constraints on Wall Street? After all, it was not Reaganites or neocons but bona fide democrats like Robert Rubin, Larry Summers and Tim Geithner who in the 1990s took apart the Glass-Steagall Act and its related legal constraints on finance, thus unleashing turbocharged financialization on an unsuspecting planet. And why did Europe's social democrats abandon the cherished principles of Bruno Kreisky, Willy Brandt and Olof Palme?

One answer lies in the transformation of global economics and finance in the aftermath of the Nixon Shock under the guidance of men like Paul Volcker.[18] The birth of America's Global Minotaur needed finance to be liberated so that the beast could do its work, supplying German, Japanese, Swedish and, later, Chinese factories with sufficient demand while also being nourished by the profits of the German, Japanese, Swedish and, later, Chinese factory owners, who poured them into Wall Street.[19]

With paper profits mounting, European social democrats and American Democrats in government were lured into a Faustian bargain with the bankers of Wall Street, the City of London, Frankfurt and Paris, who were only too pleased to let reformist politicians take a small cut of their loot as long as the politicians consented to the complete deregulation of financial markets. Franz and his mates had lending quotas to fill and no alternative other than to strike opportunistic bargains with the greatest opportunists among the politicians.

It seemed like the kind of situation that is annoyingly – at least to me – labelled 'win-win'.[20] Bankers were unshackled and centre-left politicians no longer had to wrestle the captains of industry to fund their social programmes. Financiers only had to feign displeasure at handing over some crumbs from their substantial table for the politicians to acquiesce in the logic and the ethics of financialization, suspend their critical attitude to capitalism and believe deeply that the financial sector knows best how to regulate itself.

In Homeric terms Europe's social democrats became our era's lotus eaters.[21] The lotus that made them soft and complicit with the awful practices of runaway finance was the private money-minting that Wall Street inaugurated and its international copiers scrupulously replicated. Its honeyed juice lulled them into a haze of faith where they could have their cake and eat it, where risk was riskless and where a mystery goose would lay increasing quantities of golden eggs from which the welfare state, the sole surviving connection with their conscience, could be financed.

And so, when in 2008 the vast pyramids of financial capital came crashing down, Europe's social democrats did not have the mental tools or the moral values with which to combat the bankers or to subject the collapsing system to critical scrutiny. And unlike their American counterparts, back in power after Barack Obama's victory in November 2008, Europe's social democrats did not even have the backing of a functional central bank, given the European Central Bank's straitjacket of a rulebook. President Obama, from his first day in office, had a Fed willing and able to stand by him every step of the way as his administration attempted to refloat Wall Street and clean up its mess. Undoubtedly the result of these efforts left a great deal to be desired, but imagine how much worse things would have been in the United States, and in the world at large, if the Fed had had to labour under the European Central Bank's mandate and use its tools.

Lacking the ethical, intellectual and financial weapons that they and their predecessors had willingly retired or refused to create some years before, satisfied instead with a steady supply of financialization's lotus, Europe's social democrats were ready to fall. Ready to retreat. To bow their heads to the bankers' demands for bailouts to be purchased with self-defeating austerity for the weakest. To shut their eyes to the transfer of the costs of the crisis from those responsible for it to the majority of citizens, Germans and Greeks alike, the very people that social democrats were supposed to represent.

Unsurprisingly, European social democracy went to ground, leaving the way open to racist ultra-rightist thugs all too happy to act as the protectors of the weak – as long as the latter had the right blood, skin colour and prejudices.

Decentralized Europeanization

Alexis de Tocqueville once wrote that those who praise freedom only for the material benefits it offers have never kept it long. In today's Europe those who wax lyrical about the sanctity of its existing rules are their own worst enemy and the handmaidens of discretionary, autocratic power. Europe's democrats must, for this reason, beware of those speaking of moves towards political union and 'more Europe' when their real objective is to preserve an unsustainable monetary architecture. Continuing to impose impossible rules opens the door to the ugly ghosts of our common past.

Given the European Union's history and the current state of the eurozone, political union, fiscal union and various other ideas for further centralization are neither viable nor desirable. The institutions of the European Union were designed back in the 1950s and 1960s in order to bleach politics out of them. And since nothing is as political nor as toxic as an attempt to depoliticize a political process, the result was institutions at odds with the concept and practices of a democracy.

Europeans understand this better now that the euro crisis has brought to the surface the consequences of their union's institutional design. Especially after the crushing in July 2015 of the Greek government in which I served, Europeans increasingly see the Brussels and Frankfurt technocracies as forces of occupation, a little like the French looked at the Vichy administrators. They do not want Brussels as it is structured today to evolve into their central government in response to a crisis of the European Union's own making. And with good reason.

The German philosopher Jürgen Habermas long ago recognized that capitalism has the tendency to develop a 'legitimacy deficit' – a situation in which citizens, independently of their political beliefs or ideology, lose confidence in the right of political and administrative authorities to act as they do.[22] As Europeans lose their trust in Europe's institutions, they face a dreadful Faustian bargain: accept less democracy now and more centralization tomorrow, and some time in the future you may get something akin to a federal state. Alas, accepting this deal will not bring federation any closer. Instead, it will

bolster the economic crisis and ensure the debt mountains grow taller, while further suppressing investment into a decent future; delegitimize the European Union even more in the eyes of Europeans; replace whatever democracy we have left at the national level with consultative processes that Brussels uses in order to cement a permanent commitment to deflationary, highly redistributive policies (in favour primarily of banks and

reliably of the strong and already powerful); reduce political debates on economic policy to pseudo-technocratic
discussions among unelected managers whose allegiance
lies with a technocracy created to service the interests of
the ubiquitous Central European cartel and an all-
devouring financial sector; ascribe pretend-accountability
to a European parliament, or a euro chamber, which in
reality acts nothing like a parliament but rather uses the
semblance of a parliament in order to conceal the fact
that European law is passed in the radical absence of a
genuine parliamentary process; and entrench in European law the dangerous idea that sovereignty is passé in
the era of globalization.

None of these developments is consistent with a sustainable European Union. At some point Europeans will shake
this monstrosity off their backs and escape from the iron
cage under construction around them. Unfortunately, the
resulting European disintegration will come at a horren-
dous socioeconomic cost, today's equivalent of the
generalized depression of the 1930s. The trick is to escape
the cage without destroying our common home.

The paradox of a continent divided by a common currency must be replaced by another paradox: that of
decentralized Europeanization – a rule-based redeploy-
ment of key European institutions (the ECB, the ESM
and the EIB) to attack Europe's four sub-crises while
reinvigorating Europe's national democracies. Then and

only then, once democracy has been revived at the level of the member states, can we begin the conversation that we must have about what future we want for Europe.

Meanwhile, my first-hand experience of the manner in which Europe is ruled brings to mind with renewed resonance the figure of Kapnias. His particular form of evil taught me how our loathing of democracy's worst enemies can reinforce their commitment and renew their spirit. It taught me that only steady, unwavering, dispassionate, hate-free resistance can overcome their determination. It taught me that a Greek who had never encountered a Jew – nowadays a Pakistani – could be programmed to believe that therein lay the cause of all his suffering. It also taught me that the serpent dies hard. That once its DNA is implanted into societies through the humiliation of enforced and unconditional surrender,[23] it lurks for a long, long time, waiting for a systemic crisis to spawn again.

'When I return home tonight, I shall find myself in a parliament in which the third-largest party is a Nazi one,' I told Wolfgang Schäuble in front of the gathered press during my first visit to the German Ministry of Finance back in February 2015. It was a plea for joint action. He, and the German press, took it as posturing.

Seven months later, in September 2015, after Dr Schäuble and the Eurogroup had succeeded in overthrowing our government by asphyxiating us enough for Prime Minister Tsipras to surrender, Golden Dawn increased its parliamentary representation in Athens,[24] Greece's debt reached greater heights, our society lost its will to reform itself and, most seriously, European democracy was wounded deeply. The refugee emergency that same summer, with tens of thousands of wretched souls arriving on Greece's shores, and with Europe and America's leaders bickering about how not to receive them, confirmed that Europe's integrity and soul are in disrepair.

New borders, new divisions and greater divergence is the harvest European monetary union has reaped in a continent the world had wanted so much to look up to. A continent that once produced so much light now exports bleakness and recession to the rest of the world. But it does not have to be this way. Innovative policies can combine the decentralization of power that Europeans crave with the Europeanization of basic, common problems, which they need. But it will take a radical idea to pull this happy paradox off and stop the slithering serpent. It is indeed a preposterous idea, which – you guessed it – also comes from my problematic, insufferable, brilliant neck of the woods: the idea of democracy.

To put the figure of Kapnias to rest once and for all across Europe, Europeans must regain control of their politics and their money from unaccountable technocrats. We need to take a leaf from the Americans' ideological book so as to move from a Europe of 'We the governments . . .' and 'We the technocrats . . .' to a Europe of 'We the European people . . .'

During this process it would help to extend to our continent's every corner the French triptych of liberty, fraternity and equality, amended to accommodate three fresh principles:

1. No European nation can be free as long as another's democracy is violated.
2. No European nation can live in dignity as long as another is denied it.
3. No European nation can hope for prosperity if another is pushed into permanent insolvency and depression.

Only when these principles are respected throughout Europe will the foul smirk be wiped off the faces of Kapnias's successors.

Notes

Champion of Austerity

1. It is fun to look at what a fully fledged austerity drive would
    have done to Britain's economy. Around 2010 the UK's pub-
    lic debt came to almost 80 per cent, or four-fifths, of national
    income. At the same time the UK government's total
    expenditure was about half of national income. Now, sup-
    pose Chancellor Osborne had given his pro-austerity
    instincts free rein and gone into a frenzy, slashing govern-
    ment spending by half, a cutback equal to a quarter of
    national income. Cutting this much government spending
    would reduce national income by at least a fifth. Suddenly
    public debt would go from four-fifths to four-quarters, or
    100 per cent, of national income, without even counting all
    the public money that 'had' to be given to the City's bankers.
    This is why austerity, in times of private-sector consolida-
    tion, fails by its own criteria – the consolidation of public
    debt.

2. Indeed the numbers are telling. During his first two years in
    the Treasury (2010–12) Osborne actually increased gov-
    ernment expenditure by 6.9 per cent. In this sense no
    actual austerity was practised by the Cameron–Osborne

government at all. Austerity *was* utilized by them as a cover for a substantial redistribution of spending and tax cuts that favoured the rich and disadvantaged the poor. In simple terms, the top 20 per cent benefited greatly while the bottom 20 per cent suffered even more.

The Reverse Alchemists

1. This is banker-speak for securing an interest rate somewhat above the bank's own borrowing rate and, hopefully, above interest rates charged to the bank's average client.

2. After the 2008 financial sector implosion, the banks with the most risk managers ended up in the deepest of black holes. The Royal Bank of Scotland, to give one example, employed *four thousand* risk managers and ended up needing a £50 billion bailout from the British taxpayer.

3. During 1998–2007 interest rates fell everywhere as credit was turbocharged by the shenanigans of the West's financiers. However, Germany's increasing trade surplus in relation to Europe's south and the resulting flow of money to Germany meant that the price of money (the rate of interest) in Germany was always lower than in Southern Europe.

4. The greater the supply of loans to a debtor like the Greek state, the lower the interest rate the bank had to charge to convince the debtor to take on even more loans. Thus the difference, or spread, between the interest rates paid by the Greek and the German governments shrank, giving even more incentive to the bankers to lend even more money to such debtors.

5. One way to help a stressed debtor is to reduce the interest rate charged or to prolong the repayment period without

charging additional interest. Such interest rate relief naturally reduces the value that the creditor will recoup.

6. If I write on a piece of paper 'I, Yanis Varoufakis, confirm that I shall pay the bearer of this piece of paper a sum of X euros by such-and-such a date. This piece of paper is freely transferable' to the extent that I am considered creditworthy, such an IOU has market value and could be sold by a bearer who prefers a sum less than X now than to wait until the specified date to collect X euros.

7. And when these IOUs expired, the whole process was repeated, with the banks issuing new IOUs that the government guaranteed again so they could be swapped with the IOUs about to expire.

8. The only difference between us was that I was not sufficiently motivated to keep quiet about it. But that's another story.

9. Peter Hartz, who designed these reforms, was Volkswagen's personnel director. There is a nice irony here in view of Volkswagen's implication in the major emissions scandal, which has cast a long shadow over German manufacturing.

10. Mini-jobs restricted workers to sixteen hours per week, at a standard monthly salary of 400 to 450 euros.

11. Poorer Greeks' money wages and pensions were increasing by something like 3.5 per cent, a large rise by European standards of the time, and the official inflation rate, they were told, was only 3 per cent. So their purchasing power must have been rising too. But it was not. The reason is that the inflation rate for poorer Greeks was much higher, around 9 per cent, but inflation for richer Greeks was . . . negative. Negative? Yes. If you had a mortgage on a mansion in Athens's northern suburbs, the large drop in interest rates caused by the practices of my fellow-traveller Franz and his

colleagues meant that your living costs fell! So, during the first few years of the euro, the 'good times', the Greek grasshoppers were prospering while the ants struggled. By 2010 the grasshoppers had taken their loot out of the country without paying their taxes, and it was the ants who were called upon to bail out the bankrupt state and the bankrupt banks through pension cuts, wage cuts, cuts in their health services, etc.

12. Unnecessarily. A recession that Europeans did not have to have. Allowing Greece to default and restoring German and French banks to health the way that the Swedes and the Finns had done in 1992 would have avoided this recession.

13. Data made available by the Bank of International Settlements.

14. The IMF had already developed the reputation of a ruthless bailiff, following the Third World debt crisis, the Latin American crisis and the South East Asian crisis. Ironically, at a time, in 2010, when its managing director, the infamous Dominique Strauss-Kahn, was trying to soften the IMF's image, Chancellor Merkel insisted it should be part of the troika. She needed it in order to convince her own members of parliament that the bailout's austerity conditions would be brutally imposed. Thus the IMF's makeover failed as it became embroiled in another sequence of 'rescues' that forced the weak to suffer that which they did not deserve.

15. Which was of course necessary given that the first bailout was always going to fail, being nothing more than the original Ponzi austerity scheme.

16. In the end Syriza did not win that election but came in a strong second. Its victory eventually came on 25 January 2015 in an election that I contested successfully and which resulted in my becoming Greece's minister of finance.

17. Seeing that the ECB was buying Greek bonds, the theory went, investors might have been encouraged to do so too.

18. This ploy might have worked except that M. Trichet, in a move of baffling folly, pre-announced the amount the ECB would spend on these purchases to counter the speculators. It was an open invitation to speculators to make money, as long as they could spend more money than the ECB was willing to. In Wild West terms, it was the equivalent of Clint Eastwood rolling up to the site of the showdown announcing to his opponent how many bullets he had left in his revolver. Then again, there is a simpler explanation as to why M. Trichet and the ECB did this: they only cared about making the French and German banks whole (by buying for them at full price the Greek government bonds whose value had crashed), with the story about striving to keep Greece in the money markets being only a poor excuse.

19. In the first Greek bailout, in May 2010, Europe's ridiculously hard line towards Greece was no to a haircut, no to debt relief, yes to a huge loan (€110 billion) with high interest rates. The only beneficiaries were of course the beneficiaries that the bailout had been designed to benefit: French and German banks. Once their losses were averted, Brussels and Frankfurt began to plan for the inevitable haircut, which would hit small Greek bondholders and tragically the Greek pension funds whose charters obliged them to hold their capital in Greek government bonds. So a second bailout, which included a haircut for the weak, was ratified fully by the spring of 2012. To contain the skyrocketing debt, bonds held in private hands were haircut substantially and twice – once in the spring of 2012 and once again in December

2012 – that time under the guise of a 'debt buyback'. In short, in 2012 Greece's private debt was cut in real value terms by 85 per cent. Except that the bankers and the ECB, which under Trichet had purchased more than €50 billion of Greece's public debt, were fully protected. The Greek state borrowed another €130 billion from which to infuse €50 billion into Greek banks and up to another €50 billion to pay back the ECB, which behaved like a hedge fund holdout. The only victims of the haircut were the small holders of Greek debt and pensioners, whose pension funds were effectively robbed of their capital base.

20. The first countries to violate the Maastricht Treaty rules were Germany and France, almost immediately after the euro was established. In particular, following the 2001 dot-com recession, Berlin had a choice between breaking the 3 per cent budget deficit limit, which was part of the Maastricht rules, or imposing harsh austerity upon the German economy. It opted for the former. Similarly with France a few months later.

21. Which were already issuing their own worthless IOUs with guarantees from the insolvent Greek state.

22. Through the so-called Emergency Liquidity Assistance (ELA) programme of the ECB.

23. Between 2008 and 2010, when the banks' immediate needs were taken care of by the ever-generous taxpayers, the eurozone's debt-to-income ratio rose from 66.2 to 80 per cent. Then, between 2010 and 2014, austerity pushed the zone's debt above 91 per cent of GDP. However, in the countries where the greatest austerity was imposed, debt exploded. The following table tells the sad tale of Ponzi austerity.

Year	eurozone	Greece	Ireland	Portugal	Spain	Italy
2008	66.2%	105.4%	25%	68.3%	36.1%	103.6%
2010	80%	129.7%	64.4%	83.7%	54%	116.4%
2014	91%	175%	123%	129.7%	92.1%	130%

24. This is the 'moral hazard' argument, according to which the possibility of common debt would give each an incentive to indulge in loose living.

25. So Germany would bear around a quarter of the liability as its national income was a quarter of the eurozone's.

26. Central banks do not literally print money on such occasions. Instead, every commercial bank has an account with its central bank (the Bank of America has such an account at the Federal Reserve, Deutsche Bank has one at the European Central Bank, and so on). Instead of printing cash and handing it over to them, the central bank allows the commercial bank to draw money from its accounts with the central bank that the commercial bank never deposited there – something akin to an overdraft facility. In exchange, the commercial bank hands over to the central bank as collateral some asset – for example, a stack of mortgages or personal loans that the central bank can collect on if the commercial bank defaults or goes bankrupt. The central bank's hope is that the commercial bank will then lend this money to its customers (such as companies or families wishing to buy a house or a car) with the effect of stimulating the real economy.

27. Monti had an impressive record both as an economics professor and especially as the European Commission's commissioner for competition policy. In that role he famously clashed with behemoths like Microsoft and was acknowledged as a skilled and honest operator. However, his image was tainted once he

came to be seen as Mrs Merkel's appointee to Italy's highest office despite the fact that, once in office, he acted in the interests of Italy and put up a major struggle at the European Council to bring about a proper banking union. On a personal note, Mario Monti and I have since discovered a great deal of common ground and a mutual appreciation of our perspectives on what Europe must do to overcome its crisis.

28. Ireland was felled by its banks and property developers. The tsunami of capital from Germany's banks was flowing straight into Ireland's commercial banks, which were then lending it on to developers. White elephants in Dublin's financial district, row upon row of new blocks of flats in the middle of nowhere, and second and third mortgages were the outcome. With prices racing ahead creating a semblance of homeowner wealth, credit card use multiplied and a generalized consumer spending spree occurred. When the credit crunch spread from Wall Street and London, land prices collapsed, construction workers were laid off, mountainous debts went bad and the banks themselves, the Anglo-Irish Bank in particular, imploded. In a move that will remain in Irish annals as a stigma comparable to the potato famine, the Dublin government succumbed to ECB blackmail: make the German creditors of Ireland's commercial banks whole – even a bank that was closed down and thus is no longer systemically important for Ireland's financial sector – or else!

29. See Brecht, *The Threepenny Novel* (1989), in which the following exchange appears between two characters named McHeath and Peachum. McHeath says, 'Brute force is out of date – why send out murderers when one can employ bailiffs?' To which Peachum replies, 'Admittedly, murder is a last resort, the very last – but it is still useful.'

30. The differences between Greece and Ireland are instructive. Ireland had a tiny debt before 2008. Greece had a large one. The reason is simple: capital flow from the surplus countries was directed into the Greek state, which in turn passed it on to developers – those who built highways, 2004 Olympic sites, etc. In Ireland the same capital flow went directly into the banks, which then passed it on to the developers, bypassing the state. Thus, Irish public debt was tiny while private debt was gargantuan – the opposite case to that of Greece – but when the crisis hit, the result was the same: the Irish state took on the burden of private debt and collapsed. The Greek state just collapsed.

31. Of course, a few months later, on the last day of June 2015, the ECB shut down the entire Greek banking system to force our government into accepting the troika's bailout logic. It was the price we had to pay for refusing to let our central bank be blackmailed.

32. In the case of the Irish banks, the private bonds that they had purchased were uninsured. In the case of Greek state bonds, their buyers knew that these were Greek law contracts, meaning that they could be given a haircut by a future stressed Greek government. This is precisely why the interest rates were higher than in Germany. Higher risk, higher rewards. As long as the gamble paid off, the German bankers reaped benefits that they shared with no one. But when the gambles turned bad, as Irish banks and the Greek state failed, they demanded that the taxpayers of Greece and Ireland pay up as if they had bought insurance from them.

33. No government can legally impose a liability on Jill in order to bail out Jack without passing a suitable piece of legislation through parliament. In this case, the illegitimacy of the transfer was heightened by the fact that Jack was a foreign

unsecured bond holder and Jill an Irish citizen who had never authorized her government to saddle her with a new debt (with associated cuts to benefits, wages and pensions, plus tax hikes) for his benefit.

34. The government tore up – 'retired' – the promissory notes once it took them back from the central bank.

35. As were of course Greek pension funds, except that no one really cared about the pensioners.

36. There is strong suspicion that Greek bankers lent the 10 per cent to one another.

37. See J. M. Keynes, *The General Theory of Employment, Interest and Money*, London: Macmillan (1936), p. 183.

38. Except when QE pushed the yen or the dollar down, thus helping Japanese and American exporters mop up foreign demand, adding a beggar-thy-neighbour dimension to its effects.

39. This is why in its never-enacted OMT programme Mr Draghi had to introduce, as a condition, that the country whose bonds the ECB purchases must first be put into the straitjacket of a troika programme.

40. Directed and produced by Carol Reed and based on a Graham Greene novel, *The Third Man* was released in 1949.

41. 'But to my mind, though I am native here / And to the manner born, it is a custom / More honour'd in the breach than the observance.' *Hamlet*, William Shakespeare, 1602.

Parsimony versus Austerity

1. Foreign Account Tax Compliance Act, a law passed in 2010 that obliges US citizens to report all their foreign transactions.

2. In December 2014, a month before our meeting, my predecessor had sent an email to the troika in which he proposed a series of reforms. His and Antonis Samaras's hope was that

the troika would accept these as the last batch of austerity measures and disburse the remaining €7.2 billion that Greece should have received from the troika, mostly to repay the troika. There were three major reasons why that email was ignored: first, the new austerity measures therein were too much for the Samaras government to push through parliament; second, they were too little to satisfy the troika's voracious appetite; third, a third bailout was essential to keep extending-and-pretending the state's bankruptcy, something that the Samaras government was neither willing nor able to pass through parliament given its depleted majority.

3. *The Serpent's Egg* is a film by Swedish director Ingmar Bergman. Its depiction of the genesis of the Nazi mindset among scientists had shaken me up when I first watched it as a young man.

Back to the Future

1. The Golden Dawn Party, whose deputies sat in Greece's parliament immediately opposite the ministerial box, is often referred to as a neo-Nazi party. This is wrong. There is arguably nothing 'neo' in their Nazi ideology. They worship Hitler, their symbol is a variant of the swastika, they dress like Nazis, they salute like Nazis. In short, they are fully fledged Nazis bereft of any pretence to a twenty-first-century makeover.

2. Georgia Xenou was the great-grandmother of my daughter, my first wife Margarita's grandmother.

3. By 1947, under the Truman Doctrine, the prosecution of the civil war by the West had been passed on from Britain to the United States. British troops were withdrawn and replaced by

US military advisers. The injured Xenos's torture and murder are described in an eyewitness account published in Greek. The book is entitled *The Dead Brigade*, and its author was Constantine Papakonstantinou, whose *nom de guerre* was Captain Belas. See pp. 623–4 of volume 1 (1986, third edition 2002).

4. I made this point in the press conference at the Federal Ministry of Finance in Berlin in February 2015, as part of a plea to the German finance minister and the German public to support the new Greek government's efforts to stem recession and root out the emergent Greek Nazi party.

5. After the end of the Great War, Eleftherios Venizelos, a pro-British anti-royalist republican, secured on behalf of Greece the right to administer the Anatolian coastal city of Smyrna (today's Ismir). However, soon after the Greek army took control of Smyrna, Venizelos's government collapsed and the new royalist government ordered the army to march on Ankara. Countless incensed patrioticTurks joined Kemal's army, and eventually he managed to push the Greek army into the sea. The Turks then proceed to 'cleanse' from the region millions of ethnic Greeks who had been living there since the time of Homer. In Greece that defeat, in 1922, is to this day known as the Catastrophe.

6. My references to Nazism as a serpent are due to the impression left upon a younger version of me by Ingmar Bergman's 1977 film *The Serpent's Egg* – a story highlighting the distorted pseudo-scientific imperatives behind the Nazi experiment. The title itself was borrowed from a line spoken by Brutus in Shakespeare's *Julius Caesar*: 'And therefore think him as a serpent's egg / Which hatch'd, would, as his kind grow mischievous / And kill him in the shell' (Act 2, Scene 1).

7. By the time the Red Army entered Berlin's outskirts, only seven hundred men of the Charlemagne SS survived,

fighting tooth and nail in defence of Hitler. In the last two days no more than thirty were still fighting in the centre of Berlin.

8. See W. Lipgens (ed.), *Documents on the History of European Integration, Vol.1: Continental Plans for European Union 1939–1945*, New York: Walter de Gruyter, 1984, p. 72.

9. Ibid. p. 73. Try your luck with the rest of these quotes, also taken from Lipgens's book.

i. The solution to economic problems . . . with the eventual object of a European customs union and a free European market, a European clearing system and stable exchange rates in Europe, looking towards a European currency union.

ii. The results of excessive nationalism and territorial dismemberment are within the experience of all. There is only hope for peace by means of a process which on the one hand respects the inalienable fundamental patrimony of every nation but, on the other, moderates these and subordinates them to a continental policy . . . A European Union could not be subject to the variations of internal policy that are characteristic of liberal regimes.

iii. A new Europe: that is the point, and that is the task before us. It does not mean that Italians and Germans and all other nations of the European family are to change their spots and become unrecognizable to themselves or to one another from one day or one year to the next. It will be a new Europe because of the new inspiration and determining principle that will spring up among all these peoples . . . The problem of the hierarchy of states will no longer arise. At least in its usual form, once we have cut off the dragon's head; that is, the notion of state sovereignty. Moreover, this does not have to be done outright, but can be achieved indirectly, e.g. by creating interstate European bodies to look after certain common interests (exchange rates, communications, foreign trade, etc.).

iv. [To see this federation process through], all that is required of European states is that they be loyal, pro-European members of the community and cooperate willingly in its tasks . . . The object of European cooperation being to promote peace, security and welfare for all its peoples. (This comes from a well-received, at the time, policy document that recommended the need to 'put forward a European con-federal solution based on free cooperation among independent nations [culminating in uniting Europe] on a federal basis'.)

v. We must create a Europe that does not squander its blood and strength on internecine conflict, but forms a compact unity. In this way it will become richer, stronger and more civilized, and will recover its old place in the world . . . National tensions and petty jealousies will lose their meaning in a Europe freely organized on a federal basis. World political development consists inevitably in the formation of larger political and economic spheres.

vi. It is not very intelligent to imagine that in such a crowded house like that of Europe, a community of peoples can maintain different legal systems and different concepts of law for long.

vii. In my view a nation's conception of its own freedom must be harmonized with present-day facts and simple questions of efficiency and purpose . . . Our only requirement of European states is that they be sincere and enthusiastic members of Europe.

The authors are:

i.   From a report submitted by Hans Frohwein in June 1943 to the Nazi Foreign Ministry's 'Europe Committee', entitled 'Basic Elements of a Plan for a New Europe'.

ii. Alberto De Stefani, Mussolini's first finance minister. De Stefani was dismissed two years after his appointment but remained a full member of the Grand Council of Fascism until the regime's collapse. This statement comes from 1941.

iii. Camillo Pellizzi, editor of *Civiltà Fascista*. The first paragraph is from an article entitled 'The Idea of Europe', the second from a letter by him to Ugoberto Alfassio-Grimaldi, 4 September 1943. Pellizzi was an academic who propagandized fascism and was elected to university chairs in the dubious fields of the history and doctrine of fascism (University of Messina, 1938) and the doctrines of the state (University of Florence, 1939) He survived the war's end to live the drab life of an academic sociologist.

iv. Cécile von Renthe-Fink, Nazi diplomat holding the rank of minister of state. In 1943, when the quoted statement was issued, together with Joachim von Ribbentrop, Hitler's foreign minister 1938–45, Renthe-Fink proposed the creation of a European confederacy. Under this scheme, Europe would use a single currency managed by a central bank based in Berlin. The proposed European economic and monetary union would be subject to common legislation on labour market policies and a free trade agreement. Interestingly, the greatest supporter of the von Ribbentrop–Renthe-Fink idea was Frenchman Pierre Laval. Laval was prime minister of Vichy, the Nazi vassal French state that Hitler created in the parts of France that he did not care to occupy. Pierre Laval was so keen to see France as part of a single-currency union with Germany that in a letter to Hitler he suggested including in it France's colonies so as to bring about an 'atmosphere of confidence' in the new, uniting Europe.

v. Vidkun Quisling, the notorious Norwegian Nazi prime minister of occupied Norway, whose name has become synonymous with 'collaborator'. After the war a Norwegian court convicted him of treason, war crimes and embezzlement. He was executed by firing squad in Oslo on 24 October 1945. He made this statement in 1942.

vi. Adolf Hitler, addressing the Reichstag, 1936.

vii. Joseph Goebbels, 1940.

10. This murder was the theme of Costa Gavras's film Z.

11. The reason for this is simple: eliminate local competitors to the imported goods, using the local distribution networks in the process.

12. The official rate of inflation reflects the average price increases in a 'representative' citizen's goods and services 'basket'. But the representative citizen does not exist. Put differently, she is a figment of the statistician's imagination – a creature consuming parts of each good or service in proportion to the total expenditure on these goods or services in the economy. Meanwhile, the rich get richer, and the more they spend the more the official rate of inflation reflects the price inflation of the rich. For example, in an economy of falling interest rates and increasing rents, with the rich occupying increasingly opulent houses, housing costs appear to be falling in the official statistics. The pain poorer families

face from increasing rents is bleached out of the statistics as the falling mortgage repayments of the rich grossly outweigh the rising rents of the poor.

13. The standard joke that 'when Bill Gates walks into a pub everyone becomes a millionaire *on average*' suffices to make the point that there is no such thing as an average or representative person and, moreover, when the average improves this may very well mean nothing good for the majority.

14. See Varoufakis (2013) 'The Serpent's Greek Lair' in the *Witte de Wit Review*, November, http://wdwreview.org/desks/the-serpents-greek-lair/

15. The race card was thus added to misogyny: the vast majority of prostitutes in Greece were either native Greek or migrants from Eastern Europe.

16. In the end most of the women apprehended, tested and put on display were native Greek and drug dependent. See *RUINS*, a splendid documentary available with English subtitles at: https://www.youtube.com/watch?v=9zyEegBtC1Q

17. Sweden's social democratic prime minister, in office between 1969 and 1976.

18. See *And The Weak Suffer What They Must* Chapter 3 section entitled 'That "goddamn Volcker", again'.

19. See *And The Weak Suffer What They Must,* Chapter 3 section entitled 'A timeless beast' and, for a longer treatise, *The Global Minotaur*

20. Whatever happened to 'mutual advantage'? I suppose the same people who diminished industry and devalued labour through their financialization exploits felt the need to diminish the English language too.

21. In Homer's *Odyssey* (Book IX), the lotus was one of the many impediments that the vengeful gods put in Odysseus'

path to prevent him and his men from returning home to Ithaca. It was, together with the Sirens' song, perhaps the most dastardly. Unlike the Cyclops or the menacing seas, enemies that brought out the best in the men, the lotus fruit made them soft and happy, unwilling to go back to sea to struggle towards their eventual homecoming. Odysseus had to resort to brute force to make his men return to the boats. He had to 'force them to be free', anticipating a famous expression coined by Jean-Jacques Rousseau.

22. See J. Habermas, *Legitimation Crisis*, trans. T. Macarthy, Boston: Beacon Press, 1975.

23. As Germany was in 1919 with the Versailles Treaty; France, Greece and many others after 1939, or Europe's periphery currently under the troika's watchful eyes.

24. Golden Dawn increased its seats from seventeen to eighteen in the 300-member chamber, retained its status of third-largest party in parliament and tragically became the largest party to oppose the troika's failed economic programme, thus becoming the leading opponent of a programme that 80 per cent of Greeks disdain.

YANIS VAROUFAKIS was born in Athens in 1961, and was, for many years, a professor of economics in Britain, Australia and the USA. In 2015, he became the world's most prominent opponent of austerity when, as finance minister of Greece, he refused to accept the terms of the loan agreement dictated to his bankrupt country by the Eurozone's leaders.

Since leaving office, Yanis Varoufakis has published several best-selling books about his time working with the Eurozone. This book is extracted and abridged from *And The Weak Suffer What They Must?* and *Adults In the Room*, both of which became number one bestsellers in 2016 and 2017 respectively. His latest book, *Talking to My Daughter About the Economy*, sets out to answer his daughter Xenia's deceptively simple question, 'Why is there so much inequality?'

Yanis Varoufakis is currently Professor of Economics at the University of Athens and speaks to audiences of thousands worldwide as a co-founder of the Democracy in Europe Movement (DiEM25). He is, perhaps, Europe's only motorcycling economist.

RECOMMENDED BOOKS BY YANIS VAROUFAKIS

And The Weak Suffer What They Must?
Adults In the Room
Talking to My Daughter About the Economy

Seeking some generosity
after Austerity?

Sisters
LOUISA MAY ALCOTT

VINTAGE MINIS

Friendship
ROSE TREMAIN

VINTAGE MINIS

Home
SALMAN RUSHDIE

VINTAGE MINIS

Love
JEANETTE WINTERSON

VINTAGE MINIS

VINTAGE MINIS

The Vintage Minis bring you some of the world's greatest writers on the experiences that make us human. These stylish, entertaining little books explore the whole spectrum of life – from birth to death, and everything in between. Which means there's something here for everyone, whatever your story.

Desire	Haruki Murakami
Love	Jeanette Winterson
Marriage	Jane Austen
Babies	Anne Enright
Language	Xiaolu Guo
Motherhood	Helen Simpson
Fatherhood	Karl Ove Knausgaard
Summer	Laurie Lee
Jealousy	Marcel Proust
Sisters	Louisa May Alcott
Home	Salman Rushdie
Race	Toni Morrison
Liberty	Virginia Woolf
Swimming	Roger Deakin
Friendship	Rose Tremain
Work	Joseph Heller
Money	Yuval Noah Harari
Austerity	Yanis Varoufakis
Injustice	Richard Wright
War	Sebastian Faulks
Depression	William Styron
Drinking	John Cheever

vintageminis.co.uk